DIVORCE MINISTRY

A GUIDEBOOK

Smyth & Helwys Publishing, Inc.
6316 Peake Road
Macon, Georgia 31210-3960
1-800-747-3016
©2011 by Charles Qualls
All rights reserved.
Printed in the United States of America.

The paper used in this publication meets the minimum requirements of
American National Standard for Information Sciences—
Permanence of Paper for Printed Library Materials.
ANSI Z39.48–1984. (alk. paper)

Library of Congress Cataloging-in-Publication Data

Qualls, Charles.
Divorce ministry : a guidebook / by Charles Qualls.
p. cm.
ISBN 978-1-57312-588-8 (alk. paper)
1. Church work with divorced people. I. Title.
BV4438.6.Q35 2011
259.086'53—dc23

2011022521

Divorce Ministry
A Guidebook

charles qualls

Also by Charles Qualls

Lessons from the Cloth: 501 One-Minute Motivators for Leaders
(with Bo Prosser)

Marriage Ministry: A Guidebook (with Bo Prosser)

Sessions with John and Jude: God's Abiding Words for an Active Faith

Acknowledgments

Chris Canipe and Randall Lolley introduced me to the meaningful efforts of Divorce Recovery ministry at the First Baptist Church in Greensboro, North Carolina. They caused me to enter an avenue of service that has challenged and blessed me greatly over the years.

The numerous Divorce Recovery participants have allowed me to walk a bit of life with them. In both Greensboro and Atlanta, they have blessed me along the way. All of them enter as participants; so many of them have finished as friends.

The generous members of Second-Ponce de Leon Baptist Church granted me the time and funds necessary to study for my doctorate. Larry McSwain of the McAfee School of theology and Bo Prosser of the Cooperative Baptist Fellowship walked with me through that project, which measured our Divorce Recovery ministry. We wanted to see if it was providing anything of worth to our participants. We were gratified to believe that this work has been faithful and good.

The late Bill Flanagan left us all a roadmap for how to do this work well. His wisdom and words live on. Starting in 1977, he journeyed with more than 13,000 divorced persons. He knew I was writing this book, but he lost his battle with cancer as I was finishing it. Bill will be greatly missed!

For Elizabeth, my love and my partner.
You strengthen me in ways that matter most.

Contents

Introduction ... 5

Section I: Clergy or Leaders
Chapter 1: Background to Divorce Recovery Ministry ... 13
Chapter 2: The Case for the Church ... 21
Chapter 3: Practical Matters ... 29
Chapter 4: A Working Model of a Divorce Recovery Program ... 33
Chapter 5: Perspectives for Leaders ... 41

Section II: Key Issues for Divorced People
Chapter 6: Family and Friends ... 49
Chapter 7: Personal Perspectives that Aid in Healing ... 57
Chapter 8: The Work of Divorce Recovery ... 65
Chapter 9: Forgiveness and Behavioral Patterns ... 79

Section III: Divorce Recovery File Folder
Introduction to Divorce and Marriage Helps ... 89
Divorce Helps ... 91
Marriage Helps ... 115
Worksheets ... 137
Endnotes ... 145

Introduction

One of the most frequent questions I get is "How in the world can a guy who's never been divorced know anything about what divorced people need?" That's a fair question. Choose any of my participants, and I will have to admit that I have not felt what they have felt. In the best of cases, divorce rips apart soul, spirit, home, community, and finance.

I was asking myself the same question a long time ago: what would I bring to the support and care of persons so profoundly hurting? Beginning in 1995, I have now walked with over 1,400 participants in nearly 40 entry-level divorce support groups. I've heard many stories in that time; I've felt these people's pain and facilitated moving conversations. Many of these hurting people went on to participate in second and even third levels of divorce recovery ministry. Collectively, they have become a profound part of who I am. Let me introduce you to a few of them.

"I crossed that finish line and thought to myself, 'If I can run a marathon, I can get rid of me a husband!'" So said Dominique, a fifty-two-year-old office professional, of her decision to file for divorce. If you are not a fan of divorce, you cringe at a story that begins this way. You also join the company of those who want marriages to be strengthened and to overcome even severe challenges. We share that visceral reaction, you and me. But this mother of two adult children had discovered that her husband had a secret second family. He had fathered multiple children, over a long period, with another woman. Their marriage was broken beyond the couple's ability to restore. This happens. And when it does, people like Dominique need help. Running had become therapeutic for her, but the divorce support group was a bold step.

Cheryl is a forty-year-old salesperson who had just separated from her husband of twenty years. Her children actually asked her to leave the house, so her isolation is magnified. Successful in her own career, she's okay financially. But her heart and her confidence are battered.

Darcy is a forty-eight-year-old-graduate student. Her marriage of eighteen years ended when her husband announced he was reconciling with his first wife. In divorce recovery, she realized she and her ex-husband were never really connected emotionally. She has much to unpack. She has much to learn about herself in relationships, too.

Finally, David is a highly successful professional who was married for ten years. His wife struggles with substance abuse. Repeated efforts at treatment yielded only frustration and hurt. They tried counseling to no avail. The substance abuse essentially rendered his household an unstable place for his children. He has been living on his own with the kids since he filed for divorce. He went through two levels of the divorce recovery program and then began to think about reconciling with his wife. His wife is achieving sobriety now, one day at a time. They may get back together. Although this outcome is rare, David says he's thankful for the program. "It allowed me to do the reflecting I needed to do. I learned a lot about myself and about what's been wrong with our marriage. I don't know whether we'll pull it back together or not. I do know that I'm on the road to being okay if we don't. And I know some of the patterns I don't want to repeat if we do."

These are a sampling of the stories one encounters when entrusted with the lives of divorced and separated people. My journey with divorce recovery ministry started rather inauspiciously in 1995. Randall Lolley had just brought me to the First Baptist Church in Greensboro, North Carolina, to serve as minister of adult education. Upon my arrival, we looked at my position description in finer detail. It turned out I would have an administrative role overseeing an existing divorce recovery program. Around 1990, that church had started what seemed to be the first divorce recovery group in the three-city region called the Piedmont Triad. Given that this region encompassed a metropolitan statistical area of over 1 million people, the ministry had established a broad drawing power. Even people from beyond Winston-Salem and High Point would travel to Greensboro to attend this support group.

Soon, the program offered three levels (called "Recovery," "Rebuilding," and "Reconnecting") under my supervision. Four entry-level groupings (Recovery) began in the divorce program each year, one per season. These groups averaged fifty to sixty participants each. At times, all three levels of the program ran simultaneously. When that happened, we could have as many as 120 people in the building on a Wednesday night attending a divorce support group. In this model, we relied heavily on volunteer leaders. One church member, Chris Canipe (himself a certified marriage/family therapist), was a master at keeping the entry-level groups moving forward in the program. The program generated its own leadership, as particularly well-adjusted persons were occasionally invited to join the team. Over that time in Greensboro, my role progressed to a much more direct one as a lecturer and facilitator within the program.

This experience was useful when I arrived at Second-Ponce de Leon Baptist Church in Atlanta in 2001. The church's divorce recovery program had been concluded under a previous leader. There had been no divorce ministry for some years when our current program was started. That program now reflects the upscale community. We function in more of a "boutique" style with small groups that I lead myself. The role continues to be not only administrative, but also experiential as I facilitate the groups in this two-level program.

Again, I remind you that I am always the only person in the room who has never been divorced. My participants eventually meet my wife, Elizabeth, in a social setting. They get to know and love her. In my earlier years, I was concerned that I was somehow not a valid helper because I had not experienced what my participants had. Even today, there certainly is an experiential gap that I dare not forget. Over time, though, the body of work supplants that gap in experience by providing a unique perspective. They have lived their own stories. As intense, hurtful, and life changing as those experiences may be, each is only one person's story. I have the luxury of what the business world would call "flying at 30,000 feet." My lack of personal experience is offset by an accumulated perspective. My mom's cardiologist is in her thirties and has never had a heart attack, but she has taken skilled care of my mother. My dad's orthopedic surgeon has never had a joint of his own replaced, but he has performed three such operations on my father. Quite helpfully, I might add.

For our purposes here, I will resist the impulse to state a rationale for what divorce recovery ministry is. We will get to that in a few pages. And I will put aside for a moment the wish to tell you exactly how you should set up your program. Later, you will see my model.

This book is less about how-to and more about sharing with you my perspective on the value of divorce recovery ministry. I'll offer resources that may prove useful whether you are working individually with one divorced person or leading a large group. We'll look closely at the emotional and relational issues divorced people typically face. And I will spend a large portion of the book working through issues that pertain to leaders in divorce recovery.

Someone will balk at my efforts in divorce recovery as a ministry. They will wonder how I can rationalize the investment of working with the negative outcomes of marriage. Instead, they might ask, why don't I pour myself into strengthening marriages? (I do: In a normal year, I work individually with twelve to fifteen pre-marital and married couples in five weeks of enrichment.) At the risk of all my CPE-type friends who feel that this paragraph is defensive, let me speak to that legitimate question. You can read more about my practice and my convictions in the Smyth & Helwys book titled *Marriage Ministry: A Guidebook*. In that 2004 work, Bo Prosser and I offer a treatment of our marriage ministry efforts. For instance, you'll hear about months of work poured into reaching more than 400 churches in Guilford County, North Carolina, for improved pre-marital work. I was part of a group that formulated a covenant. That pact was eventually signed by dozens of ministers in that region. They promised to require some specific investments before they would marry couples—all in the hopes of giving them a better start. Later, couples would come to me and ask if I would marry them. I would present the covenant requirements that I practiced. They would say, "Oh, you too, huh? We've run into that at two other churches already." And I would smile. Over the last twenty-five years, Bo and I have offered countless marriage enrichment opportunities between us. Yet divorcing persons need the church, too.

Still wanting to set up a divorce program from scratch? I will leave for other writers the task of creating an expansive work on how to do that. I invite you to check out the model I will set forth later. This has worked well in my settings, but it is far from the only way. The late Bill Flanagan facilitated a prolific group in Newport Beach, California. He is but one person who has authored a work that is more how-to oriented. Bill's 1994 title, *Developing a Divorce Recovery Ministry*, has been a helpful resource, as well as his occasional voice on the phone with me personally.[1] My program is heavily based on his model. Jim Smoke's fine book *Growing through Divorce* is the participant text many of us have used for years.[2] It is approaching 1 million copies sold. He is active in this work in Indian Wells, California. James Stillwell operates a large divorce program in Lexington, Kentucky. He would have much to tell you. Take *Divorce Ministry: A Guidebook* and place it alongside the how-to's. Accept that, as you start a divorce support program, you will have to allow it to evolve along with your own skill and wisdom. You will likely never stop tinkering with the program. "Ah-ha!" moments will bring changes in how you facilitate, and cultural changes may even cause you to restructure so that you stay relevant with topics or resources.

Whatever may cause you to get involved in divorce work, my dream is that you will find it to be rewarding. This type of ministry matters. Over the years, I have had people ask me why I choose to continue in divorce recovery work. All the hurt and suffering I absorb is life changing for me, too. Sometimes, wise counselors remind me to be careful about burnout. After all, I do a high volume of work with pre-marital and married couples, too. Done with intention, any of these arenas of ministry can be intense. When the church reaches out and embraces hurting people, the cause of Christ is furthered. When we have the resources with which to help, we are called to employ them mightily. So I caution you: divorce work will both exhaust and exhilarate you. I will also make you a promise: when you journey with divorced people for a time, you will rarely doubt that your effort has been spent doing God's work.

Section I
Clergy or Leaders

Chapter 1

Background to Divorce Recovery Ministry

"He's like Eeyore—only it'd be Eeyore hopped up on steroids!" That's the description of a divorcé I heard just now. As I wrote this section, my phone rang. A friend of mine called, asking me to get in touch with someone going through a bitter divorce experience. A mutual acquaintance of ours is hurting. Today is a particularly bad day for him, although it seems this person is nearly always having a bad day when we see him. The Eeyore reference is, of course, A. A. Milne's brilliantly written character from the Winnie-the-Pooh stories. This poor donkey is thought of as perpetually sad, drooping, and gloomy. He represents unstoppable pessimism and misery.

Sure enough, this real-life friend of ours bleeds his misery onto anyone who gets near him. He desperately wants help, but sometimes he cannot get out of his own way long enough to get the help he needs. He will unburden on complete strangers and then wonder why he is lonely. He wears out any nearby hope of support, chiefly by the volume of misplaced talking he does about his pain. One feature of this simple man's faith is that he confuses the nearest minister with a skilled professional who should help him in his divorce misery. Not to diminish the pastoral presence that we clergy are called to provide, but the old days of Christians seeing the nearest person with seminary training as a way of abating deep personal crises must be challenged.

When a person's hurt is deep enough or their emotional issues clinical enough, clergy must be responsible to get them to qualified helpers. Experienced though I am in working with divorced people in a support setting, this particular individual is in need of therapy for now. As I write, I am attempting to get our acquaintance to see a pastoral counselor. My call to him was an attempt to bridge him by way of referral, not to play hero with a situation that is beyond my skill level. The hope is that one day he will be healthy enough that perhaps a divorce recovery group might serve him well.

My hope is also that his faith can sustain him for the long haul. In my experience, people hurting this deeply cannot pray hard enough or read enough Scripture so that these faith disciplines alone can guide them through life's storms. One avenue of help, among many, can be a ministry like divorce recovery.

Statistical Overview of Divorce in America

Divorce in America is an issue that affects personal and family lives in many negative ways. Among the effects of divorce on individuals is a sense of separation from relationships. Divorced people often struggle with issues of trust and hope as well as self-concept. There are practical costs to divorce, such as custody and legal contention. There are often severe financial ramifications. A fifty-three-year-old female sat in my office recently. She had completed my divorce support program several years before, and I had been working with her in pre-marital counseling as she readied to remarry. She continues to struggle with trust and self-esteem issues. And, having once eyed an earlier retirement, she will now retire at age sixty in a best-case scenario. This is but one story among millions of how divorce can radically alter work, social, and emotional realities.

Statistical support might yield help in understanding the prevalence of divorce in our country. Famously, the divorce rate seems to hover just around the fifty-percent mark for first marriages. This has been true now for decades. For further perspective, a recent report from the United States census bureau shows that

- first marriages last about eight years on average.
- most people seem to wait about three and half years between their first and second marriages.
- for those twenty-five and older, 52 percent of men and 44 percent of women have remarried.
- people tend to separate for about one year prior to divorce.
- second marriages last about as long as first marriages.[3]

Diana Garland of Baylor University provides helpful background for the current state of marriage and divorce in American culture. She cites one study that suggests half of all marriages today are actually remarriages for at least one of the partners involved. Garland asserts that divorced partners find that divorce is not the solution to marital distress that they had hoped it would be. Only in one out of ten cases do both spouses report satisfaction with their lives after the divorce. The disruption of the familial relationship brings about a profound grief experience that is common even in heavily conflicted marriages. Garland also cites the drop in standard of living that women and children experience in seventy-three percent of cases.[4]

Authors Heidi R. Riggio and Jennifer E. Fite draw upon US Divorce Statistics from 2002 in suggesting that "Adults from divorced families are fifty percent more likely than are adults from intact families to experience their own divorce," a disparity they say ". . . persists when [research is] controlling for age, race, sex and parental education and income." These authors speak in terms of "embeddedness," which they define as "connections between an attitude and other units of the cognitive system."[5] Among their conclusions were that individuals with highly embedded divorce attitudes will be more likely to use those attitudes in the evaluation of ambiguous issues and specific relationship scenarios than will individuals with less embedded divorce attitudes. They also concluded that divorce attitudes are strongly related to personal relationship outcomes, i.e., that those with more positive divorce attitudes might tend to be more willing to choose the divorce option in their own marriages. Significant to their discussion was the higher likelihood that persons from a divorced family would have a lowered expectation of relationship success.

Anecdotally, I have experienced a common theme among divorce recovery participants in the areas of loneliness and disruption. A significant number of them report a need to address the impact on friendships and even family relationships due to negative reactions to their divorce. They often talk about a "choosing" that occurs among friends and families, as though money, property, and children are not the only commodities to divide as the relationship dissolves. At the very least, relationships tend to get more complicated. Family holidays, and customs are affected dramatically. Some will talk about not feeling like a part of their own worlds anymore. Some things that once felt natural now feel "coupled." One divorcé spoke for many recently when he said, "Atlanta is a tough city to be divorced in. Everybody is married in this town." For your perspective, Atlanta is a metropolitan statistical area of over 5.5 million people. Everyone is not married in this town. But from his words we get the sense of isolation and change his lifestyle is undergoing.

What Happened to Divorce Recovery Ministry?

Turn back the calendar to around 1995 or so, and you find that churches were pioneering the work of support groups for divorced and separated people. Back then, it seemed that such groups were everywhere, but now they appear surprisingly hard to find. One pastor offers candidly, "We found out it's hard work doing a divorce group. That, and churches figured out that they weren't going to gain all that many new members by offering these groups."

Still, the need is real, and there is an opportunity for the church to do far more than even the specific ministry to divorcing people. Bill Flanagan cites a George Gallup survey that indicated divergent spiritual realities.[6] While a majority of divorced people indicated that their experience drew them closer to God, a similar majority of them were unchurched. That is, they reported an alienation from their church during this time. Perhaps they perceived they might be judged or might not fit in where they used to. Many also reported a perception that the church provided aggressively for intact couples and families, but not for divorced individuals.

Indeed, divorce groups are about offering much more than they are about receiving. Is there a case to be made that validates this ministry? We'll make that case soon. For now, the discoveries made by churches in the 1990s are instructive. Like other ministries, divorce support groups do not often yield large numbers of prospects, much less converts, for membership. Institutional motivations are tough to fulfill. In today's culture, people in need are willing to come to our churches as consumers of religious goods and services. This has to be acknowledged and reconciled if we are going to move forward with divorce work. (We will address with integrity issues for clergy shortly.)

Divorce recovery programs exact a cost of resources. Even if only one person facilitates your program, there are still costs. That one person could be doing something else for the church during the weeks each year that he or she is working with divorced people. The facilitator spends time preparing for sessions or administering the start of a new group. There are also often promotional costs and facility or childcare costs associated with this program. Some will understand the ministry opportunity and value this work. Others will choose to move on to other equally valid ministry opportunities.

What Does a Typical Participant Look Like?

Paul is an old friend from earlier in my life. He lives a distance away from where I do, so we get together occasionally when he's in town on business. We also talk by phone some. He and his wife had three children together, and by his judgment they had built a good life. But she didn't see things that way. His wife left him about a year ago. For a time, they have forged a new arrangement in their small city. They share custody and responsibilities for the kids. Until now, his primary issues have been the emotional diagnosis and healing that come with relational and legal divorce. This week, though, things changed. She is newly engaged. When his ex-spouse remarries, she will move to a much larger city some hours away. The kids are to go with her. Paul's pain, by now managed in a fragile way, is freshly reopened. He is anxiously seeking counsel from trusted resources. His panic over visitation and other logistics is palpable. The heartbreak of long stretches between visits with the children washes over him like a rogue wave. For Paul, it is as though the separation and divorce have started all over again.

Interestingly, it could be tempting to think that a participant in divorce support ministry looks female and is between the ages of thirty and fifty-five years old. Paul does not fit the "female" part of the skew that many divorce groups seem to have. In order to give some indication as to what "typical" means, I will have to generalize. Over the years, I have had older people in my groups. Some of them have been divorced for a long time. I have also had participants who were so young I wondered what they were even doing being married by now, much less divorced. They really made my heart hurt. But, when I field telephone calls and e-mails from churches wanting to set up a program, they always ask me who comes to a divorce recovery group. Let me share what I have observed.

Of course, some men come to divorce recovery groups at times, but there are noticeably more women than men who are willing to be part of such a support opportunity. Flanagan, having seen more than 13,000 participants since 1977, notes this skew. Perhaps basic sociology explains this, as men might be conditioned to suffer silently. The never-let-them-see-you-cry mentality could make the possibility of public emotion unappealing. For that matter, the notion of being in a support group for something as relational as divorce might carry stigma for some men. Whatever the reasons, Flanagan and others have long noticed that there are far less male participants. In the last few years, many of my own groups have been completely female.

As for the age distribution, it would seem that fewer divorces take place before the age of thirty. For that matter, first marriages are not taking place much sooner than the age of thirty on average. On the upper end, divorces do happen after the age of fifty-five, but not as often as they do at other ages. Is this to say that I never get participants either older or younger than this age range? Of course I do. But the range I noted seems to represent the typical group by far.

Some participants come to the group when they are still separated rather than divorced. For them, and for the recently divorced people, the pain is fresh. You may journey with them as they update the group about weekly changes in court rulings, financial negotiations, and painful child custody issues. As mentioned earlier, other participants may come to the support group well past the date of their divorce. Some may be years past it. You might wonder why. I am just now hearing divorce recovery leaders whisper about a relatively undiscovered trend—that a certain portion of your participants will not come to you at the time of their divorce. Instead, they will come to the divorce support group after the break-up of their first significant post-divorce relationship. This explains, for instance, the participant who has been divorced for seven or eight years. As stories begin to be told, the group finds that his girlfriend of several years has recently broken up with him. That relationship may have started well after his divorce. The disappointment, combined with the divorce before it, finally drove him to the need for support.

There is one other factor worth mentioning. The typical participant might often be described as the "victim" in the equation. Rarely will the one who was caught being unfaithful, for instance, show up in a divorce recovery group. This could happen, but not often it seems. Participants will more frequently come in having been the one who filed for divorce. They may struggle with guilt for having "pulled the trigger" on the marriage. But, as for what they may perceive as the cause of the marriage's dissolution, participants in divorce recovery groups are less often the ones carrying the burden of blame. As most will learn eventually, there is no such thing as a no-fault divorce. The blame is ultimately spread in both directions.

What are some of the life issues that cause these participants to get divorced? You might imagine that people get divorced due to a wide variety of reasons. Some have been verbally or physically abused. They finally mustered the courage to end the cycle—and the marriage. Many of them divorce as a result of adultery. I have been surprised at the number of people who put in significant therapeutic effort to save their marriages after discovering their spouses' infidelities. It is encouraging, actually, that they at least tried. Others had deep-seeded conflict that eroded their trust and goodwill over time. Couples who wear each other out with conflict may eventually lose the will to try at marriage. Others have substance or sexually addicted spouses. Some have dealt with mental illness for which a spouse was unwilling, or unable, to get treatment. Safety and emotional issues for the entire family can take a toll in these cases. Sadly, there are still many more causes of divorce. What is the common denominator, then? Most divorces result from a slow, unnoticed emotional separation. Again, when two people lose the will to try in the marriage, a divorce begins to look favorable. I have noticed that most marriages do not seem to flame out as much as their embers simply lose intensity over time.

You and I will have exceptions to these descriptions. Over time we will encounter divorced people from every demographic and for every cause. This is merely my attempt to speak to these factors here. For readers who recoil at these causes for the split of a marriage, I sympathize. They only join me in lamenting that these people should find ways to fix their marriages. God does not desire that marriages end in divorce. Neither, though, did these couples step to the altar with a plan for their marriages to end. Yet they did end. At that point, such people need divorce recovery support as they move on into healthy chapters of new life.

What Is Divorce Recovery Ministry?

The ministry itself is offered as a "support" group that lends help to divorced or separated people, as a complement to any counseling or therapy they may receive independently. At times, participants are in the program on referral from their counseling professionals. A good divorce support group will not replace the individual work that may need to be done with a professional counselor. Instead, the two supplement each other. The divorce recovery program seeks to help divorced people gain new self-awareness and perspective within the context of a group of people who are living out similar experiences. Specifically, some elements such as story, support, skill/learning, reflection, and discussion are used in divorce recovery work.

A support group offers a safe place to those who are separated or divorced. At best, they may be receiving marginal advice from those who love them. While well intentioned, the counsel of friends and family cannot replace a support group or a counselor. When we are in (any kind of) trauma, our friends and family want the best for us. But they also want us "fixed" back to what we were as soon as possible. In fairness to them, we drive them crazy when we are hurting! Our every phone call, our every message or conversation may run on about the latest developments of the trauma. Over time, family members and friends reach the point where they feel they cannot endure "one more" conversation like that. We wake up each day suffering in our pain. Meanwhile, they live their lives in completely different circumstances. They may care profoundly, but they want us restored to normal (whatever that is!).

Central to a divorce recovery ministry is the assumption that divorce is an *exclusionary* event in life. Divorce creates not only an immediate disruption to key relationships, but also the perception that a desirable solution to marital discord comes either at heavy cost or is not experienced at all. As alluded to earlier, some even report that the union with the ex-spouse is not the only relational loss. Rather, their confidence to take risks in any friendship or family relationship is dented for a time. The perception of isolation is common among divorced people. Meanwhile, economic impacts and pessimistic relational expectations are also among the exclusionary forces at work in their lives. For those who participate in a divorce recovery program, one desired outcome might be to make meaningful connections that address the isolation of otherness.

Divorce support programs differ from place to place. Leader bias, program histories, and curriculum choices are shaping influences for groups over time. There seem to be two primary styles of program. In broadest terms, support-oriented programs attempt to provide a welcoming place for divorced people to process their experiences together. The atmosphere is shaped so that participants feel safe in sharing vulnerable thoughts and feelings. Placing oneself in the company of others who share the divorce experience should foster a feeling of companionship. In contrast, therapy-oriented groups challenge participants to share more openly. Responses about feelings, thoughts, and experiences may be debriefed at a more challenging and personal level than in a support group. Whereas "pass" may occasionally be an acceptable answer in a support group, this response is more likely to be challenged by leaders or fellow participants in a therapy group. Both styles of groups aim to help participants feel a sense of commonality and inclusion, and both would hope to help participants gain helpful perspective.

Chapter 2

The Case for the Church

Why Would a Church Offer Divorce Recovery?

There are at least three strong reasons to commit to divorce recovery work in your congregation. First, when a church offers a support experience such as divorce recovery, life needs are being met. The caveat is that needs are being met only if the group is well structured and competently facilitated. Weak, manipulative, or guilt-producing divorce work is not supportive. When done well, divorce recovery is in keeping with Christ's model of upholding those who are hurting.

  Second, churches can provide a trustworthy place for their own members and friends to receive help when divorce or separation occurs. Some of the ministries a church provides may attract community members only for a short time, but they are still brothers and sisters in Christ who need a safe, welcoming place to turn. Don't we want them to believe the "church on the corner" is the place where they can seek understanding and grace? My own program is rarely without a church member in a group. But often there is only one. The other participants are from the larger community. I am on the board of a local business and civic group. We frequently have at least one participant in the group from that body as well. The last several groups have also had at least one member from my wife's place of work. By making such a group available to the city, my church members have a group they can go to when they need it. It is a group that is sure to have enough participants for doing support work.

  Lastly, a consideration is the image a church projects to the larger community. A banner in the front yard promoting divorce recovery groups conveys much more to those driving by than time, date, and place. It may prompt passersby to consider what kind of congregation embraces and encourages those going through this painful experience.

  What good comes from participants finding a divorce support group? My doctoral project involved developing criteria by which I could evaluate and measure results from the program. I tested a willing group of past participants. Results indicated that important emotional, relational, and spiritual healing had indeed been offered. They gained a broader perspective by discussing their experiences week after week. In addition to those, the participants became a part of each other's lives. Where most of them had lived in relative isolation and loneliness, they now were part of a gathered community, and some of their connections long outlived the few weeks of the structured ministry group.

Follow-up conversations with participants who have completed the program have been encouraging. They have suggested that the ministry has allowed group members a chance to discover a supportive network of fellow divorced people. It appears that they experience trust and companionship by being together. Lasting friendships have emerged at the individual and group levels. Some groups attend significant events in members' lives, such as birthday celebrations and family weddings. Other groups celebrate holidays and reunions together. Some participants eventually ask me to perform ceremonies upon their remarriages.

A Case for Helping Ministries

In the 1980s, I began to explore my call to vocational Christian service. At my home church, I had the privilege of serving three internships as a college student. I worked most closely with Bo Prosser. Bo became a mentor and later a dear friend and ministry partner. Since my earliest days as an intern, I have heard him say that the definition of the word "ministry" is simply the act of "meeting needs."

A verse that has affected my priority for reaching out to those in need comes from Matthew 10. Jesus is instructing his disciples just before sending them off to minister in their own cities. He is, in reality, preparing them for the work of the church that will go on with—or without—Him actually there. In verse 42 he says, "And if anyone gives even a cup of cold water to one of these little ones because he is my disciple, I tell you the truth, he will certainly not lose his reward." An act like offering a divorce support group to those in pain might qualify as a cup of cold water to those who thirst. With the pain, fear, anxiety, and change that accompany divorce, the church could claim a responsibility to reach out to these hurting people. We have resources that can help them.

The Bible Speaks about Divorce and Remarriage

One of the greatest surprises resulting from my divorce work is that so many of the participants came to me curious to hear what God might think about their divorce. Even more surprising was that they expected a tough dose of judgment to come their way. At times, I have delivered a session on what the Bible says about divorce and remarriage. I must credit a predecessor of mine at Greensboro, John Setchfield, for the basis of some thoughts I have used to explore this over the years.

I often find that divorced people have heard the Old Testament messages. "I hate divorce…!" Malachi 2:16 features our God saying this with what comes across in writing as a booming voice. The Bible speaks about divorce as an undesirable end to marriage. Not flatteringly, the Scriptures also feature the use of this word "divorce" as a metaphor to describe the often broken relationship between God and humanity. Deuteronomy 24:1 begins a section that prescribes conditions for divorce in Old Testament times. The biblical presentations that specifically deal with divorce should be viewed as having a decided patriarchal orientation. Many of the teachings empowered men of that day, leaving the implication that women had less power to divorce and remarry. Mark 10:4 shows Jesus asking His disciples about the Mosaic Law, and they respond that a man was permitted to write a certificate of divorce against his wife and send her away.

Humans were created to be in perfect, divine fellowship with God and with each other. Discovering that a truly loving God had built in the freedom to live outside this perfect plan, humans eventually developed a bent for doing just that. When one reads Deuteronomy 22, the contingencies set up for divorce and infidelity are numerous. Settling on a view that acknowledges divorce as a problem on the one hand and yet communicates a Christ-like response on the other is difficult. It would seem that the greater biblical material sets a case for God's larger view of life, sin, and progress in relationships.

One recurring theme in the Bible is that God wishes for creation to be in harmony with its Creator (Eph 1:9-10): "And he made known to us the mystery of his will according to his good pleasure which he purposed in Christ—to bring all things in heaven and on earth together under one head, even Christ." The Bible speaks of all creation but focuses most of its attention on human beings because we are created in God's image and held accountable for our stewardship with regard to all other created things (Gen 1:26).

Throughout the biblical revelation, God takes the initiative to make this harmonious relationship work. The Bible indicates that God went to significant lengths to make it possible for humans to live in that kind of relationship. The Old Testament is filled with plea after plea from an angry God. But that is a God who stubbornly and redemptively calls the people to come back to right relationships. In Christian tradition, Jesus Himself is viewed as God's ultimate extension of grace. He made it possible for us not only to be saved, but also to find out how to live since he modeled goodness for us. The Bible teaches that divorce is not God's intention, but neither is murder, bigotry, lying, gossip, and backbiting—among many other dysfunctional ways to relate to others. God is equally disappointed from circumstance to circumstance.

God has tried, and continues to try now, to bring people to wholeness. God works to heal brokenness and restore people to fulfilling lives as they "work out their salvation in fear and trembling" (Phil 2:12), discovering how God would use them in the world. If one interprets any Scripture in the light of the whole biblical revelation, and through the life and ministry of Jesus, then literal understandings about divorce and remarriage are tempered by the grace of the New Testament. Stories like Jesus' encounter with the woman at the well in John 4 remind us that there is a bigger picture than our present circumstances. This does not dismiss the need for growth and reevaluation, or for new focus in our values or goals. It does not smooth over the spiraling consequences of our choices or the choices of former spouses. But the Bible does demonstrate the hope, in very human struggles, to move on and discover new and healthier ways to live.

God agonizes alongside humans in times of confusion, regret, and pain. God wants us to confront mistakes and make progress. The God of the Bible does not seem to desire that women or men be mired in unhealthy or dangerous marriages. Therefore, it would appear that the sin of divorce is forgivable and that remarriage can be within God's purposes for finding fulfillment in life. In this spirit, the works of divorce recovery ministries do not promote or encourage divorce. They do offer safe places for healing, grace, and new perspective. They make possible for many people to find a way to move forward.

Miroslav Volf's Theological Images of "Exclusion" and "Embrace"

Throughout my work, you will hear me refer to the "exclusionary" events of divorce, or you might notice that the ministry opportunities we have are understood as "embracing." This terminology borrows from the work of Yale theologian Miroslav Volf. For my doctoral work, I created a survey instrument to measure the outcomes of my long-running Divorce Recovery ministry. I wanted to see if the time and effort made a difference in the lives of participants. From the sub-themes of Volf's "exclusion and embrace" work, I developed a survey. Measuring to see if the theological themes would shed light on the spiritual and relational outcomes was a helpful way to understand the divorce recovery ministry.

As a native of Croatia, Volf had the brutal wars and genocide practices in Europe as the backdrop for many of his theological reflections. For our purposes, I will try to summarize the ways in which I have applied these themes to illuminate the work of divorce support. Although Volf has examined faith and life in terms of larger world events, his theology is useful in measuring church efforts as well. Among his many published writings, *Exclusion and Embrace: A Theological Exploration of Identity, Otherness and Reconciliation* is perhaps the definitive work.[7]

As mentioned earlier, sub-themes comprise each of the two larger concepts of exclusion and embrace. This is where Volf's work becomes particularly helpful for understanding the church's opportunities and responsibilities to walk with hurting people. His biography at the Spiritual Capital Initiative at the Yale Center for Faith and Culture states, "Miroslav has argued in many contexts for Christian faith to be seen not as an additive to help us cope with this or that problem but as a way of life. Faith, therefore, matters in all spheres of life."[8] The following is a sampling of how Volf's sub-themes apply to the exclusion and embrace of divorce.

OTHERNESS

Volf sees the biblical story of Cain and Abel as the first and paradigmatic recorded act of exclusion. He observes that the story "narrates the structure of encounter between 'them and us.' Our own ambiguities about self will fuel reactions that help us to divide society into groupings."[9] Our acknowledging of otherness is not strictly a problem. How we act on our sense of otherness determines whether or not we participate in either exclusion or embrace. Volf sees history as demonstrating an overall violent record in reaction to others. Much of the separation that happens in a deteriorating marriage results from the couple's reactions to otherness in their spouse.

EXCLUSION

In order to grasp the concept of "exclusion," one has to acknowledge "inclusion." Although the larger notion of exclusion is a focus of Volf's work, the belief that one could be excluded assumes the existence of some group that is considered to be "included." From this vantage point, Christians are considered to be a group that has the opportunity to choose inclusion or exclusion as a way to react to "others." Volf characterizes belonging to the included group a "dubious triumph" since responsibility comes with this position. He views that responsibility as becoming a person who seeks not to exclude others. Volf sees the pursuit of inclusion to be fraught with inner contradictions and views it as the struggle against exclusion.

DISTANCE

Volf draws upon biblical narratives of Abraham and Paul to mark times of "departure" in life. God called both men to leave the familiar and to engage in a new life away from what had been normal to them. This sense of leaving a familiar place in culture produces the effect of "distance." Some distance is good. Volf challenges the church to consider its complicity in that status quo by way of examining its commitment to the larger culture.[10] The church can create good distance by standing in contrast to exclusionary practices when others need grace and human company. Volf also notes the presence of exclusionary distance in life. After a divorce, relationships with friends and relatives are affected as people react to the chasm created by the dissolution of a family. Likewise, distance is created when one partner leaves the other. The view of one's place in society is also dramatically altered by divorce. The recognition of both good and exclusionary distance is important for understanding the plight of humans who hurt and being aware of the church's opportunity to aid in healing.

AMBIGUITY

Volf writes about an experience he and his wife, Judith, had while adopting a child. The mixture of feelings ranged from excitement to disillusionment. Particularly disturbing was the reality of effectively "auditioning" and being chosen as parents. The danger of being somehow rejected or deemed unworthy colored an otherwise positive experience. Volf highlights a realization that our discoveries of grace are often mixed in the ambiguity of pain, fear, regret, embarrassment, or any one of an endless series of conflicting sensations. Life is not lived under God without exposure to these experiences. Christian faith does not shield us from them, but instead adds a cherished layer of perspective and hope in the midst of them.[11] Still, we wonder "why?" Why can we not enjoy the valuable outcomes and lessons of life without paying such a steep price to gain them?

EMBRACE

Volf sees the "will to embrace" as unconditional. The starting point must be the primacy of the will to embrace another person. He says,

> Since the God of Christian belief is the God of unconditional love and the God who died for the ungodly, the will to embrace the other, even the evil other, is a fundamental Christian obligation. The will to give ourselves to others and 'welcome' them, the will to readjust our identities to make space for them, is prior to any judgment about others, except that of identifying them in their humanity.[12]

The will to embrace precedes any "truth" about others and any construction of their "justice." This will is absolutely indiscriminate and strictly immutable; it transcends the moral mapping of the social world into "good" and "evil."

BELONGING

The "drama of embrace" to which Volf refers in his works unfolds with a delivered opportunity for belonging. When humans create what he refers to as a "space for the other," they receive the opportunity to belong. Volf is clear that he is not as concerned with the cultural subtleties of physical "embrace" as with the dynamic relationship between the self and the other.[13] For Volf, the language of embrace is metaphor. For instance, in employing the powerful language of "opening the arms" Volf is focused on what causes the figurative "arms" to open. His view is that the desire for the other, wanting the other to be a part of one's life, is the important notion that leads to embrace. On a related note, he sees openness as a code for "created space" in oneself, inviting the other to come in.

PERSPECTIVE

Central to Volf's understanding of embrace is something he refers to as ". . . the open arms of the Father."[14] Volf makes a case for perspective when he employs the parable of the Prodigal Son in Luke 15:11-32. The Christian faith offers this model that gives hope. As pictured in the reunion of the long-lost son who is reconciled with his father, people are able to move forward even in the face of terrible brokenness. Volf focuses on the breached relationships within Jesus' story. After the younger son "came to himself" in the parable, a new perspective allowed for the homecoming. The father who would not let go of the relationship between them held a space in his heart open for the son. By readjusting his identity along with the changing identities of his sons, the father aided the reconstruction of relationships so that life continued in his family. Note that the older brother continued to view the younger as a non-brother at the end of the story. The father refused to be bound by that designation, instead declaring the way the family would be from that point forth. Volf points to this relational transaction as instructive for Christians who wish to be agents of embrace to people who live in broken relationships. The hope of new or renewed personhood, and inclusion, offers a new perspective.

Truth

Volf's call for honesty and accuracy in assessing life issues is helpful for churches. Rather than trying to idealize marriage, church, or personhood, a ministry like divorce recovery demands an atmosphere of genuine candor. Distraction from or rationalization of painful realities is not a healthy starting place for support ministry. In a key passage, Volf writes, "Authentic Christian hope . . . is about the promise that the wrongs of the past can be set aright and that the future need not be a mere repetition of the past."[15] This creates a genuine and open call for churches to meet life needs such as ministry with divorced people.

Volf believes the church is called to proclaim God's love as poured into the hearts of those who are "weak." Coupled with Volf's concept of "otherness," this call seems to lead naturally to a responsibility to offer ministries such as divorce recovery. One struggle for churches is to choose a stance on Volf's concept of "weakness." In the case of divorce, do we interpret the split as an example of spiritual/personal weakness or brokenness? Or do we view it as an experience of brokenness and pain that has rendered the divorced person essentially weak? One stance can evoke a judgmental or heavy-handed need to fix the participant spiritually. The other can help churches see divorced people as needing support in their life struggle and grace on the journey to healing. Whatever the case, the safety of being able to address each other truthfully should be viewed as a covenant ingredient.

Chapter 3

Practical Matters

What Does a Church Need in Order to Provide a Healthy Divorce Support Group?

In order to offer a healthy divorce support group through a church, the following components are helpful:

• *Skilled leaders* who are able to connect with divorced participants. This role need not be filled exclusively by other divorced people. Ministers, counselors, and empathetic church members can help, but they need to be open to learning from those in the group.

• A *welcoming, comfortable, and confidential room* in which to meet. Group members need to trust that their presence is not on display for prying eyes and ears. They need a room where they can sit comfortably and talk. A conversational space is best—either sofas and chairs facing each other or chairs in a circle. It is also best if the location is easily accessible from the parking lot. If the majority of your participants are from outside your church, they can make their way to the meetings with ease. Merely being there demands great emotional effort from them, so an inviting, convenient meeting place is essential.

• The *willingness* not to require certain attendance numbers or a particular level of financial support in order to justify the group.

• *Support resources* for the program, such as counselors for referrals as needed or a skilled life-transition coach. Unless you are a certified therapist, you will not likely meet all the needs your participants will have.

• *Up-front investment* in costs for training and print/electronic resources. There will also be promotional/advertising costs if you offer the program to the community at large. Participants' fees can be structured so that the church can recover its financial investment in the program over time.

• The *discipline* to resist trying to "fix" participants and their marriages. Most divorce support groups actually work from the assumption that their participants' marriages are irretrievably broken. Also, grace needs to be the predominant theme, not guilt; participants already are suffering.

- The *ability to discern leadership* among those who have completed the work so they can help others.

Challenges and Rewards of Divorce Recovery

Divorce recovery groups, and others like them that minister to suffering individuals, are not easy. They call ministers and leaders to walk alongside people who are in great pain and are often difficult companions. Leaders have to accept that they cannot save individuals from self-destructive patterns. Nor can leaders expect participants to engage in the life of the church; most never enter the church building again after completing the recovery work. Still, Christ's call to support and uphold others is upon believers who have the resources to help.

But there are payoffs. Over time, we will lead participants to powerful moments of self-discovery. Often, we will learn about life and spirit alongside the group. We will help marginalized, isolated adults find safety within a community where they may rediscover hope. For that matter, some will come to know themselves perhaps for the first time as adults. All are in a different place in their lives than they were at the time they married. To the extent that they reach clarity about who they are, they have a better chance of gradually moving forward with their lives. Last week, an entry-level divorce recovery support group in my church concluded. In that session, we focused on the powerful effects of our families of origin. We delved into the formative experiences that shape us and examined the adaptive behaviors that we employ in relationships. We talked about the way in which we all engage in patterns of relating. Toward the session's end, heads nodded as one young person said, "I wish I had known some of these things about myself before I married! He and I both would've stood a better chance." She is only beginning a personal journey of discovery, but she is now hopefully armed with greater emotional and relational self-awareness. These tools help unpack what has happened and forge new ways of growing into future love.

Some members will find their way into the broader life of the church after having initially ventured in for divorce recovery. Pam is a young mother of three. She signed up for divorce recovery at our church. Her children needed something to do while she attended her group. Pam let them participate in the mission and choir groups we offered for their ages. The kids immediately loved what they were doing. When their mother finished her entry-level divorce group, Wednesday nights at the church had become part of their lives. The kids continued attending, and Pam found a pew she liked to sit on near the front in worship on Sundays. She is now a volunteer in one of the choir groups and in their Bible study class on Sunday mornings. She has recently signed up to go through the level two session, "Divorce Rebuilding."

One other story reflects the growth and self-awareness that can happen in a good support group. A new group of divorce recovery participants was scheduled to start class. The leader was finishing his time with participants who were in an advanced level of the same program. One gentleman in that program told the leader, "You go down there next week and tell those folks that we said they're going to be okay." Others nodded in agreement. The next week, the leader passed that word along to the entering class members. Eight weeks later, as they closed out their time in the program, the same leader asked them what they would tell a new group. Darcy, whose husband decided to reconcile with his first wife, responded, "You tell them we said they're going to be okay." Surprised, she added, "Hey, that's what the other group told you to tell us!" And so it was.

Chapter 4

A Working Model of a Divorce Recovery Program

Many of you have perhaps made it this far in the book because you are searching for answers to "how-to" questions. What would a real divorce recovery program look like? I provide my model only as an example. Perhaps you will be underwhelmed by what you see, since I cannot recreate everything that happens in a typical group. On the other hand, others may read this and be overwhelmed in that they will not consider themselves ready for such a demanding role. Each of us led a group for the first time once. Allow yourself the creative freedom to be informed by the presentation of this model. Let this section spark the design questions that might lead you to the best model for you and your group.

The design of these sessions draws closely from a model that was in place at a previous congregation, the First Baptist Church in Greensboro, North Carolina. The weekly sessions last one and one-half hours. Two main components facilitate the weekly divorce support experience: (1) group viewing of video content and (2) group discussion of the weekly topic as assigned from the book they read between sessions. Advertising includes church publications, print ads, church web site ads, a printed brochure, and a large banner in the church's front yard. Additional word-of-mouth referral from past participants has also been helpful for our program.

Session 1: Introductions and Program Overview

On the first night, participants receive a folder of resource materials. (See Section III.) A letter of welcome is included, as well as an overview of the program. Viewer guides that correspond to the main outline of video content are included for each session, along with potential discussion questions. Various articles on relationships and divorce that I have written or compiled are also included. A page discussing the potential of a divorce recovery experience is available as well. Additionally, there is a helpful article titled "The Bible Speaks on Divorce and Remarriage."

Group members are supplied with a copy of Jim Smoke's book *Growing Through Divorce*.[16] They are assigned one chapter to read between sessions. Each session's video segment features Dr. Bill Flanagan speaking on the material from the assigned chapter. Flanagan is a minister to single adults at the Saint Andrews Presbyterian Church in Newport Beach, California. His biographical information included with the videos summarizes his contribution to the field by indicating that since 1977, he has conducted Divorce Recovery Workshops for over 13,000 people. Flanagan earned a Master of Theology degree from Princeton Theological Seminary and his Doctor of Ministry degree from Fuller Theological Seminary.[17] Intermixed are brief video clips of his own participants in their small group discussions of the same material. Each week's video segment lasts about twenty minutes. These particular videos are no longer available for retail. I will eventually transition my sessions to part lecture/part discussion.

After a short break, the groups move into discussion for the remainder of the session. Although the assigned topic provides the framework for each week's discussion, I am careful to allow a chance for participants to discuss how their week went or especially any interaction they may have had with their former spouses or family members. My job as facilitator is to guide the transition from this discussion toward the topic for the evening. This requires sensitivity, as the personal debriefing of their weekly lives forms a living curriculum and is arguably as important as the assigned material. One could allow this kind of random discussion to go on each week and never address the material. The leader should attempt to help members to support each other, yet achieve some interaction with the assigned material. It is important to balance between general discussion and reviewing the material.

In this opening session, participant introductions consist of individuals sharing their names, occupations, how long they were married, and where they are in their divorce experience. Responses typically range from newly separated to as much as five years divorced. At this point, I generally ask participants to discuss why they chose to come to the divorce recovery group. If the introductory discussion seems to be on pace with our overall time limits, I may ask them to respond to the question, "If you had to explain to a friend what you believe happened, how would you do it in three or four sentences?" Before we end the session, I always offer them another way of telling why they have come to the group by asking them what they hope to get out of the experience. These questions allow group members to participate somewhat on the first night, while also generating hope for what such a group can accomplish together.

Group members are told in the opening session that "pass" is an acceptable response to a given question if they are not emotionally prepared to discuss it. However, they are encouraged use the pass sparingly so as to challenge themselves toward meaningful self-revelation and into the safe help of group mates. With group discussion, open-ended questions are asked and responses come randomly from the group as opposed to starting with a participant and then moving in a linear fashion around the circle.

Part of a leader's skill is in not cutting off a participant's discussion before he or she has a chance to speak thoughts or feelings reasonably. I do work to prevent one participant from dominating discussion at the expense of others. At times, I also have to be skilled in pulling some of the more reticent participants into the discussion without embarrassing or unduly compelling them. Additionally, my facilitation has to include careful guidance when group members might get overzealous in trying to pry or pull a response from fellow participants. Occasionally as leader, I negotiate the delicate moments when a participant might disclose at a level that is inappropriate even for a confidential support group.

Participants are also encouraged to recognize the value of socializing before and after meetings. No weekly topics are likely to be explored fully for their satisfaction. Either to dialogue further, or to develop relationships with other group members, social time together generally happens after sessions. This is important since the support experience is enhanced for most of them by building trusted friendships during the eight weeks.

Session 2: Is This Really Happening Me?

In the second session, I welcome participants and immediately start the first video session. After a short break, we begin introductions. This allows latecomers to join the group and still have everyone get to know each other more. The practice also allows each participant the chance to relax and have a first video topic in common before the social component begins.

The first video session explores general topics such as objectives for the series, myths about divorce, and stages of the divorce experience. Stated objectives include facilitating new friendships, practicing mutual need therapy, sharing struggles with fellow strugglers, understanding the divorce experience, and destroying some myths about divorce. As for the general topic on the stages of divorce, the video draws from Elisabeth Kübler-Ross's death stages, as they provide a useful parallel to the divorce experience.

Following the video, group discussion begins. To start, I ask them to respond randomly to what they have heard. As remaining time allows, group members are asked if they have connected with a particular myth about divorce. Later, I ask them whether they are able to identify which of the stages they may be in currently. These questions help group members tell portions of their stories or reflect on what they have learned thus far from their pain.

Session 3: Assuming New Responsibilities—Planning for Yourself and Your Future

The video segment for session 3 begins with a presentation of two basic marriage types: dependent and interdependent. This material assumes that while dependent spouses lean almost totally on the other for support, interdependent spouses maintain uniqueness in their togetherness. The video transitions into a presentation on assuming responsibility. Participants are challenged to assume responsibility for their part in the failure of the marriage, for their present situation, and for not projecting future success onto someone else. Finally, participants are challenged to take responsibility for themselves. One key point is that humans cannot be responsible for the happiness of others, including their spouses. This is often of great interest to participants and generates helpful discussion.

In the group discussion following this video segment, participants are asked to react to the notion of taking responsibility for their part in the failure of their marriage. Over the years, I have found this to be a difficult task for some participants. Since so many enter divorce recovery viewing themselves as "victims" in their marriages, the discussions tend to be lively. Then I ask them to name areas where they feel they might need to grow, as well as any barriers that might hinder that growth. As time allows, group members brainstorm practical steps they could take to facilitate personal growth.

Session 4: Coping with Your Ex-Spouse—A Relational Reality that Continues to Exist

The video for session 4 points to four possible levels of relationship with the ex-spouse: (1) ongoing and continuing contact, (2) contact that exists because you are parents, (3) memories of a relationship that used to be but does not exist now, and (4) a relationship unresolved because the former spouse is no longer living. Participants will hear that the emotion of hate guides a person until they are consumed and even burned out. Likewise, they are cautioned that while the legal processes of divorce may be necessary, one rarely ever gets satisfaction in the courts. At some point, they must learn to cope with their ex-spouse in ways that are not destructive to self or others. From this transition, they are led to consider eight kinds of divorce. The video highlights these divorce types from Smoke's book. They cover divorce circumstances ranging from change to conflict and from relational pressures to no-fault. Finally, the video offers practical steps to recovery.

In beginning the discussion of the video, I ask participants to select the cause for their divorce with which they most identify. They are encouraged to explain why they identify most with that particular cause. Then they move to discussion of current feelings toward the person they once loved. They are also asked how (if at all) this might contrast with the way they wish to feel about their ex-spouse. As time allows, we discuss what they might be able or willing to do in order to improve their way of coping with the former spouse.

Session 5: Being a Single Parent/Becoming a Whole Family Member

This session demands sensitivity to the group's makeup. The topic requires that we find a balance between sensitivity to parenting issues and the awareness that some participants do not have children. Whether parents or not, their personal understanding of family is dramatically altered by the divorce experience.

In the video, Flanagan begins with a discussion about single parenting. He acknowledges "overloaded [emotional] circuits," resentment, perception of a lack of respect, and a feeling of being trapped by the duties and emotions. He then offers eight guidelines that single parents might find helpful. These guidelines touch on role responsibilities as well as warnings about misusing children in the fight against an ex-spouse and overindulgences with the kids while acting out of guilt or envy. The video then transitions toward a broadening of the family concept. Flanagan points out potential positive experiences that can emerge from the terrible circumstances of divorce. These include opportunities for new personal discovery and growth, freedom, new concepts of partnership with kids, new friends, and even spiritual development. Negative experiences are also noted, including loneliness, loss of structure, guilt, and pressure from some family members.

In discussion, we often begin with debriefing how participants' families were altered by the divorce. Changes in relationships, feelings, schedules, and other challenges will normally surface. We seek to have group members identify any positives that may also be resulting from their divorces. I then guide the group to discuss a broadened concept of family. We seek to identify sources of family in our lives. The group members leave having been challenged to identify one or two family-building action steps they might begin to take. These are listed on the board as they respond so that group members can see others' thoughts and be informed by them.

Session 6: Finding and Experiencing Forgiveness—Discovering a New Family

The video content for session 6 offers challenges and perspectives on the issue of forgiveness. Participants are helped to consider what they have normally believed about the nature and practice of forgiveness. They frame this new perspective against the intensity of the experience they are presently living. Among others, the video suggests these points:
- Forgiveness is crucial for healing to take place.
- Forgiveness is giving up all claims on the one who has hurt you.
- Forgiveness is surrendering your right to hurt back.
- Freedom is found in risk.

Dr. Flanagan discusses consequences that happen to us when we don't forgive and then discusses several contentions about what forgiveness is. He then proposes practical action steps toward forgiveness that are specific to the divorce experience. Of significance is the notion that forgiveness is a need for most divorced people. This notion challenges the seemingly more obvious issue of forgiving the ex-spouse. The idea behind this is that participants are ultimately able to control only what they feel within themselves. As they struggle with issues they may need to forgive of the ex-spouse, they are balanced by the awareness of their need for self-forgiveness.

Discussion in this session is generally rich. By this point, participants are normally comfortable with the process and with each other. The intense feelings brought about by "forgiveness" often yield a valuable conversation. The leader can ask questions like these that help participants move through the discussion: "Where are you in the struggle to forgive yourself?" "What are some things for which you might need to forgive yourself?" "If you have asked your ex-spouse for forgiveness, what happened?" Discussion turns toward the nature of forgiveness, with emphasis that forgiveness is less an event in time and more a mindset or attitude to be lived over time. If time allows, discussion might turn toward evaluating the consequences of not dealing with forgiveness issues.

Session 7: Thinking about New Relationships—Relating, Dating, and Mating

Video content in this session follows up on the book chapter by discussing dimensions of mature relationships. Participants are asked to evaluate their patterns with regard to the speed of relationships, the quality measures of relationships, and relational depth. Then they are helped to recognize quality in relationships by considering confidence (trust), communication, commitment, criticism, community, and change. While this alliteration of terminology might distract some people, the basic outline yields relevant information.

I begin this discussion by pointing out a portion from the book on "fears" of divorced people as they enter new relationships. I then ask for reactions to Flanagan's discussion on mature relationships. I ask participants to consider the potential effect of "urgency" on relationships, since many divorced people feel a need to rush back out into new love. I also introduce for their consideration the transition of a mature relationship from the functional realms of "recreation" toward "responsibility." Of emphasis is the romantic need to balance these two relational needs. We discuss the influence of sex in adult relationships and pursue biblical as well as relational cautions about sex.

Session 8: Relational Patterns and the Influences of Families of Origin

This final session serves as a potential "graduation" point for divorce recovery participants. The entry-level divorce recovery program under consideration for this book is programmed for eight weeks' duration. Some few participants will elect to conclude their participation in divorce recovery at this point. Having successfully completed the initial eight-week program, many others elect to continue in a second divorce recovery level, also lasting eight weeks.

As a final session, this meeting is oriented toward application and moving forward with life and love. As the second of two "live" presentations, it begins with me addressing the issue of families of origin and their shaping effects. Then we move into a presentation on living in relational patterns.

This material is influenced by Harville Hendrix's work that led to the "Imago Therapy" movement within counseling.[18] For a time, these sessions were presented by professional counselors at Second-Ponce. Due to these particular counseling colleagues moving their offices out of Atlanta, I have begun to offer these presentations myself.

Participants are challenged to consider their particular adaptive behaviors. They are also made aware of theories that conclude that our marriage roles and biases are formed at an early age as informed by the way we view our parents. Even reactions against these roles and biases are shaped by their influences. Divorced people are encouraged to evaluate how their backgrounds may lead them to attract/be attracted to particular personality types. They are also led to consider how they generally participate in significant relationships. In order to alter some of the patterns they feel might work less helpfully than others, this journey toward awareness should be a helpful start. Discussion ensues within the presentation, and the entire one and one-half hour session is interactive with participants. Questions that shape discussion toward the end might include these:

- What have you learned about yourself at this stage of your divorce?
- What would a healthy relationship look like if you realized you were in one?
- What are some realistic goals you have for yourself in a new dating relationship? In a new marriage?

At this point, we acknowledge the pause in participation that many will have as they may plan to move forward within part 2 of the overall program. Because of this, most will see each other again in a matter of weeks as that program begins. For everyone, we acknowledge that this support group experience has concluded and that they have the assignment of living out their divorce journey constructively. I pledge my availability to the group members as a minister and resource for them.

Chapter 5

Perspectives for Leaders

Lessons Learned

I can still remember the first time I walked into a room to observe a Divorce Recovery group in action. The year was 1995. I expected it to be the darkest, most depressing room I had ever entered. My assumption was a level of collective pain, probably injurious to anyone who wandered too close. Honestly, I was intimidated. I almost felt unworthy to enter a place where help was so profoundly needed.

Instead, what I found there was an outpost of the kingdom of God. It was a unique place where hurting people were finding community, safety, and understanding. The weeping, wailing, and gnashing of teeth I had expected simply were not there. Inside that room, I found people who looked just like the ones I passed on the street every day. They looked like my family members and church members. Bound by the divorce reality they shared in common, they were a pleasant lot to meet—not at all the image I had conjured up based on my fears about what the intensity of this experience must do to people.

Over the years, I have learned many lessons about divorce ministry. Doubtless, there is a lifetime's worth of lessons I still need to learn. But for these few pages, let me walk through some of the impressions that stand out to me.

(1) Divorce recovery is a vital ministry. My sense of call would be incomplete at this point without this ministry. Let me be even clearer: no other work I do is more fulfilling than the small steps of progress we make each week in the divorce recovery group. Many Wednesdays, my work can be as hectic as it is on any other day. I may bounce from visit to visit and from meeting to phone call. My day can change completely if someone encounters an emergency that requires my help. The difference on Wednesday is that I occasionally find myself thinking, "If I can just make it until Divorce Recovery, I'll be in a comfortable place then." This ministry

has evolved from being an intimidating assignment to a place where friends meet to do good work together.

(2) Divorce recovery as a ministry is not static. My program plan and my skill set keep evolving. There are things I used to build into my facilitation plan that I simply don't do anymore. Those items have been replaced by new questions, more urgent exercises, or a trust in the discussion process to take the group where it needs to go in a given session. I find that I am probably far better at this work today than I was fifteen years ago. That makes sense. One should hope to do something long enough to develop new competencies along the way. You will not design your support group ministry and keep facilitating the group in the same way. You could, I suppose. But as insights and experiences build, it is helpful to continue to strengthen the way you guide group members to new discoveries.

(3) The culture changes, but the core issues of divorce recovery participants remain fairly similar. I now minister in a different city than the one where I began divorce work. The two cities differ in noticeable ways. Also, 1995 was a different place in time than 2010. Cultures change, and group dynamics change. But the circumstantial, emotional, and relational needs of separated/divorced people hold steady. You may have to change the ways in which you promote the program, and you may begin to hear slightly different backgrounds to the stories each time you convene a new group. Even as you move with the changes in the world, though, you will also be glad for a firm beginning foundation.

(4) Each group has a unique personality. Your challenge each time is to have the skill and emotional versatility to work with your current group. Divorce recovery support is not automatically a weekly session in which the mood is profoundly painful and dark. On the contrary, the mood seems to brighten for most groups week by week. Also, not all groups start out in deep outward pain. I doubt that any two groups I have had would be similar to each other in personality. Some can be downright fun! One group that came through the program years ago still gets together for bowling and other socials. They invite Elizabeth and me to join them when they get together. Others have gone to each other's weddings, and even their kids' weddings, because they became friends outside the meeting room. Still other groups struggle their way through, and you sense that they will part on the last night for good.

(5) There is a sacred trust in a divorce recovery support group. I have developed an appreciation for a participant who is willing to walk through the door into our meeting room. Truthfully, the people who choose to attend

a divorce support group are the healthier ones. While they bring their fears, tears, and sneers with them, the act of showing up is a sign of health in most of them. The truly unhealthy are the ones who cannot make themselves come and get the group support and fresh perspective that might move them forward. They are coping in a variety of other ways. For those who attend, always remember that this was not easy for them to do. Your participants are placing their hurt and hopes in your care. I have come to realize that their presence is not to be taken for granted.

(6) Some participants will never be ready to conclude a divorce recovery support program. At some point, however, they must graduate and move on. This will sound more negative than I intend, but the analogy is the mother bird who pushes her young from the nest. She trusts her instinct that it is time for them to fly. Clearly, some people become "addicted" to attending support group meetings. Their emotional and social needs are being met. At Greensboro, I added a third level to the program that focused more intensely on what a future romantic or married relationship might look like. This was partly at the request of program leaders and participants. I was proud of that third level in the ministry design. We made it something that served a fine purpose. Here in Atlanta, I only offer the two levels. For some, four levels would not be enough. Still, they should finish at some point. If you choose to add to any ministry program, you must have a good reason to do so. Ensure that the need belongs to the ministry itself and is not for your own satisfaction.

(7) Occasionally, you will have to serve as a protector. Some people may inquire about the program in order to come meet "available" people to date. If you remain alert and aware, you will catch on to most of them in their inquiries. It is part of your responsibility to protect those who attend your meetings from others who would take advantage of them. Sometimes, people will call me and ask about re-enrolling. They tell me what a positive experience their group was for them. I turn them away politely. I want everyone to be in a divorce recovery support group for the same basic reason and to enter on level ground in their experience.

Support Group versus Therapy Group

Many counselors run what might be called "therapy" divorce groups. They are often heavily dependent? on group "discussion." In these groups, people can join at whatever point they desire and exit when they feel ready. These groups might take place year-round and usually meet weekly. Facilitated by the professional counselor, these groups are open. Vulnerability and risk awaits the participants, as these groups plumb the psychological depths of their issues. It may be well in-bounds for the facilitator or fellow participants to push someone to share beyond his or her comfort level. When led by a skilled person and composed of willing participants, this is a fine way to do divorce work.

By contrast, most "support" groups also facilitate group interaction. However, the answer "pass" is always acceptable, and the culture of the group respects the boundaries as perceived by the individual participants. Since support is the goal, the notion is to blend presentation of material with group conversation. Safety, acceptance, and the sharing of stories and new perspectives are the primary goals. The programs I am most familiar with are in this support category. My own certainly are, and I would not consider myself skilled to lead a more "therapy" styled group. For the remainder of this section, our focus will be on the support type of divorce group.

What are some planned outcomes? In a divorce support group, we never simply gather to talk. There might be people who would prefer that. You have seen the model of my program in chapter 4. There is a plan for each session, and participants hear a small amount of material each week. That, plus the video clip we watch, comprise about an hour of group interaction. A resource book supplements the published text we use. We do this in the hopes that group members will have a particular kind of experience that includes the following aspects:

• Acceptance. When so much of their lives may be in a period of perceived exclusion, divorce support provides a group of people with whom they can identify and feel comfortable.

• Confidentiality. On the first night, we stress the importance of confidentiality. Group members need to feel free to say what they feel with the knowledge that everything that happens within the room will stay within the room.

• Safety. As much as divorced people talk about their crisis with family and friends, it is likely that they filter most conversations to some extent. The support group is a safe place where there is grace to be honest and open. We are there, first and foremost, to talk about the reality of divorce.

• Commonality. Although the specific circumstances in their marriages may have differed, the participants can count on being in a room of people who share the end result. Their parents, coworkers or friends may never have been divorced. These fellow participants have. Such a community is invaluable.

- A "mirror." The principle of not being able to see the forest for the trees is in play with divorce support. Sometimes the other participants and I provide a large degree of objectivity for the divorced person. While they were once lost in their pain, they will often rediscover that there is more to their lives than their divorces.
- New knowledge. In a divorce recovery support group, we can share relational insights and personal and psychological awareness. Participants walk away having learned something about how to process their experiences.
- Relational awareness and confidence. Friendships and group membership reawaken personal confidence for many participants. They come into the group and find that they really can be loveable. They are of value. Sometimes, friendships deepen enough that they remember that the risk and investment of love can pay off after all.
- Fresh perspective. New realizations about oneself are among the best outcomes of these groups. Participants need to get to know themselves as they are now, not as they were some time ago. They need to put their former marriages and their divorces into context so that other aspects of their lives can become more apparent again. They need the reassurance that new chapters of life lie just ahead.
- Hope. One of Volf's elements of "embrace" is the genuine narrative of hope. While eight weeks is certainly not enough time to recover, the discovery of hope can take place in such a group. For those who move on through the next eight-week group ("Divorce Rebuilding"), powerful encounters with the sense of hope are even more likely.

Section II

Key Issues for Divorced People

Chapter 6

Family and Friends

What Friends and Family Wish Divorced Loved Ones Knew

There is often a disconnection between the divorcing person and his or her loved ones. First, let's admit the obvious: the only ones who can live the experience firsthand are the divorced people themselves. Although I refer to this as obvious, support group participants often seem oblivious to that fact. When one is in the moment, perspective can be lost within the intensity of the pain. Most divorced people probably have many things they wish they could convey to their family and friends. Likewise, family and friends may not be able to express precisely what might be helpful for their divorcing loved ones to know.

In this section, we'll explore some of the basic dynamics that are often at work. Sometimes people know what to say once the awkward and painful struggles end. At other times, the words are never verbalized, but both parties might have been helped if someone had spoken up.

The following discussion will not be exhaustive. Each person's experience is unique, as is that of his or her loved ones, but there seem to be basic issues that could be addressed as soon as they surface. Family and friends might want a divorcing/divorced loved one to know several things:

- *"We are grieving with you."* Many hurting people try to block off the pain in their lives. In an attempt to manage those who care about them, they may say something like, "This is my own problem. Don't make it yours." Or they might try to shield their family and friends from their pain. In some families, a divorce can become the proverbial elephant in the room. The pain hurts everyone, but no one has been permitted to name the obvious. Here is the reality for most divorced people: immediate family members in particular are grieving also. This is a reality and not a choice. They, too, are disappointed that the marriage did not survive. They, too, have to get their hearts and minds around the death of a relationship that might have once seemed so promising. They can't be shielded from the pain. They are already experiencing it.

There are parts of this experience through which one must travel alone. But there are also emotional pieces of the divorce experience that eventually need to be discussed. Remember the sheer power of hearing a divorced person express aloud feelings or thoughts that have thus far only existed as internal matters. Loved ones need to be permitted to talk about the divorce in the same way. Of course, divorce will not be the most pleasant of topics, but the freedom of opening up about the subject may result in a level of support for both sides. As we have already mentioned, families and friends can catch too much of the pain. But too little open discussion is just as harmful. Rather than be spared this pain, family and friends of a divorced person must be allowed to draw support from each other.

- *"We are working through some stigma as well."* This part of the divorce seems awkward to mention, but it is real and needs to be named. The family may not only hurt for the person going through a divorce, but they might also share some of the other emotions. They may struggle with local scrutiny of what happened. They may carry some social stigma or embarrassment.

Again, one could choose to say that this is none of their business, but it is their business on some level. No mother or father enjoyed the day of a child's wedding ceremony with the thought that the marriage would end in divorce. Some family members may think, "Divorces happen in other families, not in mine!" Few people are callous enough or jaded enough to accept a divorce in their family in stride. Because of my work with so many divorced people, I am also frequently approached by their parents, siblings, and even friends. They, too, are looking for books to read or web sites to visit. They, too, are trying to get their feelings in check. They want to do something to relieve the hurt they feel about the end of a dream.

For the purposes of this book, I name this dynamic not to add to the pain of the divorced person but to acknowledge the real social impact that results from a divorce. At some point during the support conversation, this topic may surface. The divorced person and his or her family might be aided by openly addressing this topic at least a few times in order to name their feelings accurately. What they do with these emotions is important. The grace they grant each other is vital in healing. Pretending that the pain of divorce is limited only to the direct parties is false, no matter how well intended. People experiencing divorce must allow their mother or father to grieve. I counsel the group participants that by being as open and gentle as possible during this part of the journey, they can ease their parents' pain.

Eventually, all parties will adjust to some extent. Other details will become more important in time. All of this is part of what most people refer to as "moving on."

- *"Our advice is intended to be helpful."* Certainly, many of them are handing out poor advice. Although open dialogue is important, too much talk can wear out even a caring listener. Loved ones know how to relate to the divorced person under normal circumstances, but this level of pain has brought about a crisis mode that they are unsure how to address. Frankly, they do not know what to do with a loved one who is so broken. Their well-intentioned hope, for many reasons, is to fix the divorced person—soon!

I am thinking of one mother in particular. I watched her adult son go through a painful divorce. As far as anyone knew in this family, his was the first in memory. This mother's relational style has typically been to rule the family in a powerful matronly role. Her direction of holidays and family gatherings is precise and detailed. True to form, she rendered the former daughter-in-law into a "villain." Her need to throw down cushions to break the family's emotional fall drove this posturing. The divorce was seen as the young woman's entire fault, leaving the son as an obvious victim. This framework was preached as soon as it was clear that the marriage would end. With that perspective, it seemed that the son needed to do little if any true evaluation or personal discovery. Although he followed his instinct and did some private reflection and support work, he soon bought into his mom's message: the divorce was, relatively speaking, not really his fault. He bought her next message as well: the true solution for his pain was to hurry back out and fall in love with another young woman. The idea was to get on with life quickly, thereby "ending" the hurt. He did so, and one hopes that the second marriage will go well. Time will tell. Often, though, such speedy "recoveries" don't go so well in private. Much painful baggage gets brought into the next marriage, still largely unprocessed.

The advice of loved ones is well intentioned, but that does not mean friends and family members know what is best. My counsel to divorced people is to be aware of the source of their technical and emotional coping strategies. I advise them to filter them through common sense and professional help. Take in the gift of the loved ones' concern, and bank that love in their emotional reserves. But they also should be ready to draw a line as to how prescriptive they allow these voices to be in their journeys. Even with the best of care, some biased and grieving loved ones can still steer them wrongly.

- *"Sometimes we get weary of hearing of your divorce!"* I can still recall a painful confession from a mutual friend. We had a loved one who was going through a career crisis. The solution to the ill fit between job and person played out over a protracted period. In the interim, a few individuals were the recipients of soul-rending complaint from the one who was searching. Close friends and family members found this to be the only topic the hurting person seemed to talk about. All the while, our own lives were moving along. We had other pressing matters, including joys and fulfillments in our families. The painful moment came when one of us said aloud, "I've gotten to the point where sometimes I see him coming and I literally just walk the other direction. I love him, but sometimes I just can't take one more conversation about how bad his life is."

Those who are swept along in the wake of a divorce within their family or close friendships often experience this dynamic. While they genuinely care about the people involved in the divorce, they truly can hear too much about it. Earlier, I pointed out that sometimes the lines of communication need to be opened between divorcing/divorced people and their loved ones. This notion makes that no less true. But the point earlier was to stress that untapped support may be waiting on a specific aspect or subtlety of the divorce to be admitted and opened for discussion.

On the other end of the spectrum comes this tidbit that family and friends might like to scream, "Your divorce is not the only thing happening in the world!" In fact, it's not even the only thing happening in the divorced person's world. Those who care about the divorcing person want them to remember this. They would simply like to talk with them about other things, along with the occasional talk about the divorce. The divorcing person is still welcome to come to their child's concert, ballgame, or birthday party. Celebrating the bright moments of loved ones' lives will demonstrate some regained health. I also counsel group participants that loved ones would remind them that they are not their divorce. This is not all there is to who they are, nor is this the final chapter of their life. Loved ones are available to listen and talk about the struggles. Divorced people earn the personal capital to do that with them by remembering that all of life continues to march on. Perhaps loved ones might say, "Talk to me about world headlines, share with me how things are going at work, or ask how I'm doing now and then (that is, continue to be a true friend), and I'll have enough fuel in my emotional tanks to help fuel your journey as well!"

- *"Let us be a source of fun, perspective, love, and enjoyment!"* Family and friends can help powerfully their divorcing loved one retain that broader perspective. They want to play, relax, and spend time with their divorced friend. Sometimes, in pain, the divorced person may pull away from the support systems they need most. Or, as mentioned previously, they may say too much on the phone or in an e-mail and wear down even those who love them most. But, in reality, the schedules and social habits of the divorced person may have been dramatically altered in response to the pain and horror. As often as possible, divorced people need to nurture balanced relationships with their loved ones. They need to draw from them the full range of gifts that good friendships offer. Too much fun and distraction will not speed up the healing. On the other hand, having unconditional love from enjoyable people goes a long way.

Family or friends stand by, waiting for their divorcing loved one to plug back in. They want to help him of her in the journey back toward a fuller life. In fact, I encourage divorced people to see their existing relationships as a part of their lives that may need new investment from them. I encourage them to rediscover who they are in this chapter of life. This is not to be mistaken for an ill-fated attempt to retake the life they used to live before their marriage and subsequent divorce. That will not be realistic, especially if the marriage lasted several years. The people and places of their former (or "single") life changed during the time they were married, and they must move forward. Finding out who they are now and reconnecting with their loved ones more deeply is an important part of this experience. Further, successfully reinvesting in existing relationships will help them regain confidence in their ability to love and relate to others.

Many of the same dynamics that make a successful marriage, for instance, are not exclusive to marriage. Relationship with parents, siblings, and close friends needs to feature many of the same traits. Trust, sharing, risk, reward, honest disclosure, and more are essential in a healthy relationship of any kind. Skill sets like conflict resolution, negotiation, and creative problem solving are the foundations of a healthy marriage. They also take place between family and friends. Encourage group members to exercise what may have become a somewhat neglected state of relational *fitness*; encourage them to love, risk, and grow again!

What Divorced People Wish Friends and Family Knew

- *"I wake up most days thinking of my pain first."* The alarm clock goes off. A tired, worn out figure stumbles toward the bathroom. He stops by the mirror and takes a look: "You're a mess," says the voice belonging to the face in the mirror. "Okay . . . just breathe for now." Especially in the early stages, many divorced people report this as one example of a successful start to any day.

- *"My separation or divorce is all-consuming."* Friends and family would be amazed at the load the divorcing person carries. They know about it, but they can't truly understand unless they've lived through the experience themselves. Even then, they've only lived their own unique experience.
- *"The clean break you want me to make with my ex-spouse may not happen."* If there are children, then child-custody issues will likely link ex-spouses long after the divorce is finalized. In fact, Jim Smoke cites eleven "life realities" that will probably bind ex-spouses for as long as they both live. Some of these include seeing or not seeing the former spouse, talking to or not talking to them, is financial support paid or not paid, are there good memories or only bad ones? In all, his realities suggest some ties to the former spouse that will cause struggle for some.
- *"My emotional pain over the failure of my marriage is intense."* Friends and family know a divorcing person is in pain, but they cannot know exactly the nature of that pain. They may not understand the struggle to process social or spiritual stigma, or that their divorcing loved one may face insecurity regarding prospects for a future love. I advise group members that loved ones do not want to see them carry this heavy burden, but they cannot wish away the consuming grief. While it is important for them to realize the depth of the pain, it is also important for loved ones to understand that they cannot fix the situation.
- *"I know I talk about my experience too much, but the power of hearing thoughts and feelings leave my mouth is healing."* Family and friends need to know that divorcing people do not enjoy talking about their pain, but they need to verbalize it in order to tap into the power of the words themselves. More than likely, they do not expect loved ones to fix their problems. Talking repetitively about certain issues is a vivid sign that they simply need to express those thoughts or feelings aloud. They need to be heard.
- *"I don't need friends and family to 'fix' things for me as much as I need safe people with whom I can be real."* Friends and family can be sources of support without feeling responsible for making everything better. Sometimes I say, "Loved ones must understand what you *do not* need from them." Some of those things may be

> (1) A quick, easy fix that might not be relevant or real. No less than Albert Einstein is supposed to have said, "Every problem has an easy solution. Most of them are wrong." Friends and family must put aside their need to fix the problem. Instead, they should offer an active but

listening ear. When they try to solve their friend's problem without being asked, they may eventually push that friend away.

(2) Judgmental reactions. Perhaps the friends or family genuinely disapprove of the ways in which their loved one is coping with his or her divorce—a new lifestyle, a decision about what strategies to take, a method of handling a crisis. The divorcing person may may need them to serve as counsel for some things, but they may forfeit that role if their reactions are too judgmental. It is especially easy for parents to come across as judgmental (unwittingly). They may say, "You don't need to feel that way!" Even with the best intentions, their words may call into question whether they are safe or real enough that the divorcing person can share and disclose with them in confidence. Instead, loved ones might say, "I know you feel _____. Tell me more about why you feel _____." Words like these validate their message in an open-ended manner that is devoid of judgment.

(3) Doing something with what they hear. This goes beyond offering suggestions or unsolicited advice. In the quest to end the hurting, some loved ones will spring into action. They will have conversations and do things they think are helpful. They will threaten, beg, and cajole on the behalf of their divorcing friend or family member. Adult children who are divorcing want parents to know that they might prefer to act for themselves.

- *"I need to express my emotional state. I know some of my feelings may scare you, but I need to talk about them."* I encourage participants to accept that their feelings are real; they are a window into where they are right now. However, feelings are not up for negotiation. In fact, a therapist or counselor knows that feelings are neither good nor bad. Feelings are neutral. Feelings simply are! Only when we act upon them do value judgments begin to apply. My loving mom still sometimes insists, "Honey, you shouldn't feel that way." But I do. Her not wanting me to have a certain feeling does not make my feeling any less valid.

- *"I know you'd like to spare me this experience and its pain, but I need to go through it in order to heal."* Friends and family should resist the temptation to try. Even the horrible feelings, the vivid memories, will be catalogued as a part of the human experience. Since these events have happened, divorced people needs to process the aftermath fully. Doing so will help them eventually work toward resolution, adjustment, and closure. As they grow from these negative experiences, they will be forever changed as human beings, often for the better due to the lessons they have learned. Perhaps they will move forward, break some of their negative patterns, and not repeat the same relational mistakes again.

Chapter 7

Personal Perspectives that Aid in Healing

Helpful Levels of Awareness

Earlier, we looked at how "perspective" is one of the outcomes a divorce support group can facilitate. Most divorced people understandably become lost in their own experience. The scope and depth of their pain is overwhelming. They are often awash in logistics, whether legal, financial, or something else. What levels of awareness might be helpful for a divorcing/divorced person? Here are a few.

• *Their divorce is not all of who they are.* This experience appears to be so encompassing that many divorced people forget who they are. They can assume a dark outlook on life, fueled by the notion that their divorce defines them. This is not really a conscious choice. Instead, this state slips up and overtakes them. In a support group experience, they can sometimes rediscover that their divorce does not totally define them. Just as their marriage was only a portion of their identity (albeit a significant portion), so their divorce is only part of who they are.

• *Emotional neutrality about their ex-spouse is the desired outcome.* Christians in particular might focus on the ideal that all divorced people can one day have some version of a restored relationship with the ex-spouse—maybe even a friendship. In reality, the best and most sound outcome might be to return to emotional neutrality. In other words, there was a time before a divorced person knew her spouse. Therefore, she had no feelings about that person. A return to a place where that person is not a source of hurt—or love—in one's life may be the best outcome to expect. This does not ignore the ways in which the two divorced persons may be interconnected for the rest of their lives, but if they are no longer absorbing emotional energy from each other, then they are at least neutral. Fortunately, there are some exceptions in which ex-spouses are good friends; more realistically, however, neutral is better than painful.

- *This painful time will come to pass, not come to stay, for life is lived in chapters.* Sometimes, divorced people cannot see an end to this difficult experience. As I write, one of my most recent participants has signed her divorce decree within the last week. She has endured fresh emotional pain in completing this symbolic/legal act. However, she also points out a new milepost. Signing the legal documents signaled to her that one day, her season of darkness might lift. For her, that was a powerful dawning. She is not there now. The more eternal forces of life and spirit will have to deliver her forward. Divorce is not to be downplayed; this chapter in life is more awful than most people ever envision. Still, it is good to remember that new chapters lie ahead. Perhaps even the best ones yet!

- *They confuse the legal system with a place where they can find satisfaction.* Bill Flanagan says this most clearly. Divorced people owe it to themselves to take care of their business, legally and financially. They need to stand up for themselves and fight for the best divorce arrangements possible. But they will never find satisfaction in the legal or financial arenas. Healing, hope, and newness are found in places other than the courtroom.

Aloneness vs. Loneliness

Aloneness is valuable. This is one of the key discoveries I have made since beginning my work in divorce support. I had never realized the power of the alone time I have experienced in my life to this point. Whether we are children or adults, aloneness is a valuable part of our human experience. In this state, we are freed of the distractions and noise of life. We can question, rehearse, debrief, and think. We can listen to the voices of others and to the soundtrack of our own experiences.

The trouble is that divorced people often experience a painful adjustment that is forced by loneliness. The changes in household arrangements and relationships caused by the separation force this loneliness upon them. Even people who have reported abuse and pain at the hand of their marital spouse still feel lonely when the marriage ends. Loneliness causes a different set of voices to play in one's head. Self-doubt, pain, and fear are often the soundtrack of loneliness. None of us enjoy loneliness.

What can we do about loneliness? How can we help divorced people through this painful reality? I believe we serve them best by helping them to distinguish between these two look-alikes: loneliness and aloneness.

When I was a young adult, I was chosen for a coveted internship at my college. I took one semester off and was sent out to represent my college. Specifically, my assignment was to visit almost ninety high schools spread across half of our state. I was in a car by myself for most of three months. I lived in hotels, ate alone, and was responsible for the schedule and business issues of my travel. Parts of each day were spent driving through the gray of winter in rural south Georgia.

At first, these weeks and months felt lonely. Away from the fun and noise of my roommates, I experienced too many quiet hours. I had to adjust to the relative anonymity that was mine apart from my appointments in the high schools. I had to watch out for myself for the first time. Early on, there were times when I felt sorry for myself. But months later, I began to realize the value to that time apart. In doses, I asked questions about myself and answered them. I assessed what was important to me and reflected on a new chapter about to begin as graduation loomed. I started to make new plans. I found that I was fairly at peace with myself, even if this kind of work was not something I wanted to do for the rest of my life. In the end, the alone time was more beneficial than disturbing.

In working with divorced people, we should be ready for opportunities to help our participants make the distinction between aloneness and loneliness. We cannot wish loneliness on them, but we can hope they embrace the gift of aloneness. During their time alone, they can do a more forensic debriefing of their marriage experience. They can reconnect with who they have become at this point in their lives. They can assess where they have been and what may lie ahead. In alone time, they can also take stock of what is important to them in a relationship. They can notice what some of the deal-breakers and dealmakers might be in a new love.

What "Recovery" Might Mean: A Case Study

In his book, *The Unwanted Gift of Grief,* Dr. Tim VanDuivendyk offers the following exercise.[19] If someone from another culture asked you how to eat using a fork, how would you explain it to them? Lest you think the answer is easy, Dr. VanDuivendyk's exercise stipulates that you have no fork with which to demonstrate. Do you still think this conversation would be easy? Think it over. You have no way to show the person how to eat with a fork; you only have words. Well, that and your hands fumbling around trying to make some sense of how to eat.

Sympathize with me as I attempt to set forth in this section what "recovery" might look like. I have only words. There is no specific person whom

I can literally set in front of you as a demonstration, although I will shortly offer one person's testimony. For now, your own story will have to do, or the story of someone with whom you journey in divorce support.

No one is in a humorous mood on the first night of a new divorce recovery group. Tensions can run fairly high as the group assembles. Participants tend to come in cautious, at best. However, one of the early chuckles is likely to be at the acknowledgment that "recovery" probably won't happen in an eight-week support group. Even those who haven't wanted to acknowledge this to themselves seem to laugh at the idea of such rapid healing. Everyone senses that recovery is more of a marathon than a sprint. In their lifestyles, though, some people are more likely to admit this to themselves than others. If figuring out how long the journey might take is tricky, it is even more complicated to define what divorce recovery actually means.

Hear the voice of one whose signs belie a level of recovery. Gale is a mother of two girls. A popular, attractive girl in high school, she was married at a young age. The union lasted for over twenty years. She has raised her children and managed to put herself through college in the years since the divorce. She exhibits a toughness to which what she has managed to accomplish attests. Gale remains attractive and has a sharp wit. Had it been her goal, finding a new man to marry quickly would have been too easy a solution. Fortunately, she has chosen the more extended path of recovery.

She observes, "I've been divorced for eight years. They have been the hardest years of my life. Yet they have offered me a greater understanding of myself. I wouldn't have that gift had I not gone through the difficulties and pain over the past few years. Sometimes hardship can be a blessing."

Now Gale is doing something that is tough, initially, for many who have been stung by divorce. She is finally opening herself to the likelihood that she will one day love again. "I'm actually starting to soften up to the idea of marriage," she says. "I think that is only because I know what my needs are now. The key is finding someone who can be sensitive to those needs *and* for me to be able to fulfill their needs. It's a delicate balance, but I want to believe it can be accomplished."

Then she adds this thought: "The best thing about the last eight years is knowing that even if I don't find him, I will be just fine. God still has a purpose for me and my life, regardless of my marital status. Although . . . ." She trails off with that last word, which portends a hope grounded in eight years of hard work and reflection. It hints at the openness to another relationship someday. But what else can we hear in Gale's words? Let's learn from her.

- *She didn't waste the time that has passed.* However long the painful period of decline and separation lasted in her marriage, the divorce has now been final for eight years. She has had the passage of time. There are no shortcuts to recovery. Those who love a divorcing person want them to be better soon! The person wants healing for herself, too. The myth that "time heals all wounds" begins to lead us in the right direction, but the fact remains that time itself is no healer. Time well spent is tremendously healing, though. Notice that Gale acknowledges the hardship of those years. I will take her at her word that the past eight years may have, in fact, been the most challenging of her life in some ways. But perspective has become her ally. In that time, she has opened to new self-awareness.

- *She is not the same person now as she was at the time of the divorce.* Certainly, she is not the same person she was when she married. She has taken the chance to get to know her self anew. One of the early lessons should be that when one emerges from a marriage (even of a few years), he needs to get reacquainted with the person he is now. There is no return to exactly the way you were when you got married.

- *She realizes that she experienced transformative growth within the wrappings of horrible suffering.* This is a life reality. We can try to rationalize life, spinning the hurtful circumstances of divorce toward something that is supposed to sound good. Most divorce support group participants won't have patience with this behavior. You may render yourself irrelevant if you insist on trying to make their divorce into something better than it was. In the end, great damage has been done. Still, from that pain can emerge clarity and newness once the person does intentional work in his life. In Gale's case, she found new self-awareness and understanding, something she refers to as a "gift."

- *She will likely love again.* Among Gale's evolving awareness is that she may, one day, share a place in her heart with someone again. This time, though, that relationship will need to be more mutually nurturing. I am rarely happier for my participants than when they come in saying that they will never marry again. Assuming they are serious, I can hope that they are at least momentarily focused on themselves and not on getting back into the love game. I rest in the statistical likelihood that they will, in fact, remarry one day. For now, though, we work on their personhood. Gale has taken some time, and along the way she has discovered some up-to-date things about who she is.

- *She has learned what her own needs are now.* If heeded, that kind of awareness can help one evaluate a potential partner in a more mature way. It is not that Gale will want to terrorize every male with her new shopping list of perfect traits. However, if her knowledge is used rightly, she does know herself better now and can evaluate a potential partner in that light. A mature person can sense a relationship that has a legitimate chance to be healthy because of such knowledge. Likewise, an even more mature person can end a relationship that is headed nowhere.

• *She will frame her life, moving forward, exclusive of her marital status.* If Gale remarries, fine. If not, then fine too. In my program, participants have a moment when they hear Bill Flanagan's words, "Plan the rest of your life as though you will never get married again." Although they probably will, it helps when divorcing people are forced to consider themselves apart from a spouse. There is an irony here that is as true for younger, never-married people as it is for our divorced friends: at the point when we least need a marriage partner, we are probably at our most ready to have one.

In short, Gale indicates an understanding that God's purpose for her life is a larger notion than her marital status. She has rebalanced her life. She has worked, parented, and studied. Along the way, self-reflection has happened. You should not hear me suggesting that everything is now "fixed" in Gale's life. She still has challenges. Unmistakably, though, Gale is not where she was when the divorce happened. By many noticeable indicators, she has made it to the "adjustment" phase of her painful new reality. In other words, she is healthy enough to move forward with her life.

Powerful Questions that Guide the Journey

Divorce is both event and process. To define a divorce as simply a legal or custodial transaction is to deny the human portion. Documenting the legal, financial, and even relational happenings is fairly easy. One of my recent group participants spoke of the "boxes" of documents that are stored in her basement. With gusto, others nodded their heads in acknowledgment that they also have similar boxes. But to document the emotional issues and happenings of a divorce is a different exercise altogether.

I get amused when people ask me technical questions about divorces. Over the years, I have picked up a rudimentary understanding of how one gets a divorce. I have some basic understanding of the parties, time lines, laws, and proceedings. However, those are hardly the reasons anyone comes to me when they divorce. Sure, we chitchat before sessions about the latest court development or financial realities. We relax for a few minutes each week as group members arrive. I'll often find them already in conversation, or I may ask, "So what's new this week?" For those who are separated but not yet divorced, discussions about practical matters sometimes ensue. They find listening ears and even helpful advice when they share what has happened with the lawyers or negotiations. That's a beautiful thing to watch.

Thankfully, though, that is not what most of my participants show up wanting to talk about. Long after the legal ink has dried, the hardest work of most people's divorces is just beginning. This is the part that demands a deep journey inward. The questions of the heart, the experiences of the spirit, and the woundedness of the soul become the more pressing agenda in divorce recovery.

Questions are central to the recovery experience. A lot of these explorations yield energy and exhilaration. Along the way, gratifying discoveries can happen. However, some people resist the questions. They know many of them will lead down dark, threatening emotional alleys. And they are correct. I encourage them to take these journeys in doses. There are basic themes that seem to repeat themselves. Some happen by way of my asking questions to spark discussion. Others happen along the way as divorced people talk with each other. There is no way I can list such questions exhaustively. Here, I will attempt to capture many of the most common ones. I will list the questions for our consideration, and then I will offer thoughts on what role they play.

- If a friend asked, how would I describe what happened to dissolve our marriage?
- What was my personal measure of error or causation in the split?
- What have I learned from this experience so far?
- Who am I now, at this age and in this stage of life? How might that differ from who I was when I first married?
- What about my past do I need to grieve?
- What aspects of who I am do I need to claim and celebrate?
- What are some mistakes that I need to own up to and learn from?
- What might it take for me to love again without making the same mistakes?
- If my divorce is only a part of who I am, then who else am I? What other parts of me exist beyond the end of my marriage?
- If I were in a healthy relationship, how would I know that?
- Who are the people in my life that are most important to me as a person?

Again, these are by far not the only questions one might need to process. They are simply a few of the basic questions that help one along the journey through a divorce. To be sure, these help measure progress as one moves farther from the divorce events. Depending on how the answers expand and change, recovery may be happening for an individual.

I have some additional observations about these questions that might be helpful. For instance, these questions are misused or misunderstood if they appear to be a *checklist*. One could take this list and think that having a response to any of these will indicate a milepost to check off. Marking enough of them from the list might eventually hint that one is "recovered." Sadly, that would be missing the point. Instead, the *journey* with these life issues is the point. Short, succinct, and easy answers reveal a denial. More reflective, honest, and mature answers show that a person has reached a new place since the divorce. Another important notion is that this list is only as relevant as a person's personality and relationship are unique. That is, each divorced individual will have his or her own questions that might be added to these. Such questions arise from the awareness that is brought about when a person is finally confronted with himself or herself.

Chapter 8

The Work of Divorce Recovery

Grief Work in Divorce Recovery

In Jim Smoke's book, *Growing through Divorce*, a powerful lesson comes early: the realization that the grief of divorce is similar to the grief of death. Bill Flanagan highlights this in the first video session that supports the book by Smoke. In my work, I offer support groups both for those who grieve a death and for those who grieve the end of a marriage. Over the years, I have come to support Smoke's notion. These two painful life events leave the survivors facing a similar emotional pilgrimage.

A divorce is, among other things, the death of a marriage. The covenant a couple has undertaken together is being rendered void. The oath they sincerely pledged did not hold up. A love that was intended to last forever has not survived. Relationships are fractured, and child custody is thrown into uncertainty. Holidays and celebrations are altered. Friends and family members will not relate to them in exactly the same way. Possessions and places will be divided. This produces a powerful mourning for most people who experience divorce. In baseball, we are taught to get up and "shake off" a minor injury. Divorce pain is no minor injury. People cannot quickly shake off the death of a true marriage. A model for understanding this journey might be helpful to some.

Perhaps the most accepted vehicle for understanding the grief pilgrimage is Elisabeth Kübler-Ross's work titled *On Death and Dying*.[20] In her study, she worked with dying patients for an extended period. Their reflections on dying gave her the basis for understanding the journey of our grief. I believe her work has been misunderstood and perhaps misused in some ways. The misunderstanding may come from the assumption that she had actually done more work with loved ones after the deaths of the patients. But, these understandings of grief came before the death event itself. The patients' grief reflections shaped her work primarily. Still, this work has carried powerful lessons for most of its readers, who are probably more likely to work with the bereaved than the dying.

For me, the misuse of her work is more critical. In hearing her five "stages" of grief, we often develop a *linear* understanding. That is, we can be lulled into thinking that these grief stages represent a flat, predictable passage from a mythical "point A" to "point E." Reading about each of these five stages, we tend to view grief as a series of mileposts. If we feel that we can check each off as we pass them, then after the fifth we think we should be done, finished, healed, or graduated because we touched all the figurative bases! This is not so.

In reality, those who have genuinely grieved will likely report a messier and less predictable path. When we grieve, we are not apt to move past one stage irretrievably on to the next. Instead, just when we think we're "done" with one grief task, a life circumstance or memory may pull us backward to revisit a stage or task again. In divorce support, we see this happen when a participant has had a rough phone conversation or e-mail exchange with her former spouse. Some bit of new information or insensitive behavior will take her backwards emotionally. We may move back a stage or two to one we thought we were long finished with. The dying or bereaved might ask, "Why am I feeling this? That is so silly? I've already felt that!" Or the divorced person might say, "What is wrong with me? Why am I crying about this again? I thought I left that in the past."

However, the one who allows himself to grieve is moving forward over time. Grief work must be done. It is part of the human experience. I tell bereaved people and divorce support participants that if I could shelter them from this experience, I would not. Or, if I could somehow remove this pain from their paths, I would not. Some of them ask me why, and I share my convictions about the role pain plays in our lives:

• Grieving is part of living. If you can grieve, you are alive. You are healthy and even normal.

• Grieving is a price we pay for taking the risk of loving. We cannot love deeply and then not mourn the loss of the one we have loved. When I see a couple divorce and not experience a painful emotional journey, I am clued in that they might not have loved so deeply in the first place.

• Grief is one of the filters through which we process the human experience. Alongside joy, love, and appreciation, grief is one of the ways in which we evaluate where we have been so far.

• Grief is one of the bearers of life's lessons. No matter how devastating your pain, grief will not leave you as you were. Some of the damage may not be completely undone, but the wisdom that comes with it will inform how you see life moving forward. Much of it will serve you well.

For now, let's examine the stages of grief as Kübler-Ross proposed them.

(1) *Denial and Isolation.* Denial gets a bad rap from most of us, I think. It is true that it is unhealthy for a person to live in perpetual or extended denial about any reality. But Kübler-Ross described this temporary state of "shock" (denial) as a defense mechanism. We are given the gift of this defense to cushion the blow of devastating news. In this stage, we may act as though the loss has not happened. We may truly not connect with the reality. Those who love a grieving person should not be fooled by that person's denial. The person is experiencing loneliness and isolation. Jack Snell was a wise pastor who served Baptist churches in the Southeast. His early death caused widespread grief for many of us. Jack once said, "I am not in too much of a hurry to kick denial out from under someone in grief. It may be the only leg they have to stand on at the moment."

(2) *Anger.* If denial's statement is "That can't be!" then anger's question is "Why me?" Jo's husband was a fixture in their church. His death came due to an accident at his home. No one foresaw his loss, even though he was not a young man. He and Jo had been married for almost sixty years. To those who knew them, they were inseparable. It caught some people off guard when Jo spoke candidly to those standing around her at the funeral. "I'm so mad at him right now I don't know what to do," she said. And inside myself, I mumbled, "Good." Why? Because it clued me in that Jo knew with finality that her husband had died. I am sure Jo has gone back in some ways and revisited her brief denial stage at times. She and I have talked about the fact that we "can't believe he's gone." In fact, she told me, "Sometimes I start to say something to him, or laugh about something, and then I remember that he's not there to talk with me." Still, her frustration with him in that moment meant that she knew he had died. Anger is an emotional reaction toward the one who has died or an emotion generalized toward the death itself.

In any event, it marks the awakening to a reality of loss. The "why me" feeling is frustrating to process. Those of us who do not want our friends to be in pain might counter with, "Oh, don't feel that way." We mean well, but we only end up sending the signal that we are not safe people with whom they can be honest. If someone is grieving and they admit anger, we must remember that their feeling is just that—their feeling. Let them process the anger so that they can move forward.

(3) *Bargaining*. Kübler-Ross felt that bargaining for brief periods was a helpful stage for those who were dying. A common reaction is to try to strike some sort of deal that might keep the inevitable from happening. The singer-patient with a malignancy prays that she might take to the stage and give one last grand opera performance. The aging ballplayer dreams of one more at-bat in which to hit a homerun. In divorce, the equivalent might be Steve. He walked into one of my early divorce recovery groups convinced that his wife would soon return to their marriage. For weeks, he went through the motions of attending the divorce support group. His heart was not in it. Then one day, he pulled me aside. "I get it now," he said. "She's not coming back. I've got to find a way to deal with my realities in light of that, don't I?" His bargaining had been focused on the better husband he would try to be or the leeway he would grant her to have greater freedom in their relationship. He had focused on all the ways he would be willing to change if only she might return. He would be a different man, the man she wanted him to be. Bargains are often made silently with God. They are a way of working out guilt and disappointment.

What emotional good can bargaining serve? This one is fairly simple. Bargaining allows us to continue staving off the full reality of what has happened for a time. It also allows us to set up specific expectations by which to measure that reality. One by one, as our bargained conditions go unmet, the dawning occurs. This loss has actually happened. This is real in my life! My relationship is not going to return to its original state. In fact, the relationship is not going to return at all.

(4) *Depression*. I watch my parents' generation respond to the word *depression*. For them, this word is not to be uttered aloud; something more like a whisper is used. And clinical depression is no laughing matter. This discouraging and dangerous state of mind must be diagnosed. Unmanaged, dark possibilities come to life. I watch my people of faith struggle with the realities and helps of clinical depression. They fear that this is somehow a sign that they lack salvation or God's love. Treatment, therapy, and often medicines can do marvelous work with clinical depression.

But Kübler-Ross rightly points out that some level of depression is to be expected in grieving. An older woman was dealing with a new diagnosis of heart trouble. She had experienced a serious onset of symptoms that hospitalized her for a time. A deacon in her local church, she spoke in hushed terms. "The doctor told me that I might be depressed." She spoke of feeling comfort at seeing me nod and agree that some small measure of depression was likely at the moment.

For many in grief, depression is non-clinical. The pain is profound and real. Kübler-Ross sees this kind of depression as a tool. The bereaved one is building a bridge toward yet another stage. The cause of depression is that the reality of loss is becoming apparent to the one who grieves. The awakenings that produce this state will mature. The lasting affects of this depression give way to new realizations of acceptance. There may even be a couple of different states of depression for those who have lost something or someone. The first might be louder and more expressive. There is much to say aloud about the pain. In the second grief, Kübler-Ross sees people moving on to a more reflective and quiet state. Divorced people find value in a support group because it gives them a safe place to express and process the depressing truth.

(5) *Acceptance.* If a grieving person is given enough time and enough support, he will reach a more neutral state. He will neither deny nor be as angry about the inevitable. Acceptance implies that there is "adjustment" to the new reality. Even this stage takes time. Acceptance will happen one insight or one discovery at a time. Layer upon layer of wisdom piles on until the grieving person sees the journey differently.

Acceptance signals that the hurting one is ready to move forward. This is not to be confused with everything being "all right now." There is no need to rationalize just to make the divorced person feel better about her new reality. There does not have to be anything good made of the terrible divorce. I have no conflict with acknowledging the problem of divorce that has led to the growth of the new reality.

Some divorced people who have grieved their marriage's end will remarry eventually. Their love for the new spouse may be genuine. This next marriage may feature much greater health than the first one did. The partnership can be sound and the romance exhilarating. Still, they might wake up now and then feeling a tinge of regret about their former marriages. They might miss something specific about their former spouses. Is this a signal that there is something wrong? Or is this the human experience with grief and healing? Acceptance has moved them forward to a place where they have made room for a new love and a new life. But is the former marriage completely forgotten? No. Healed significantly? Perhaps so.

How does this discussion help the divorced individual? The understanding that what they are going through is probably something that can be called "normal" is healing. Sometimes participants bring many life issues into a support group that are summarized in one basic question: "Am I the only one?" Not to minimize what they are experiencing, but we get the chance to reassure them that they are not alone on the journey of divorce grief. Another question may be "How will I cope?" Due to the variety of your participants, your group may often be surprisingly helpful answering such questions. Powerful things happen as expressions of grief make their way into the support group.

Sometimes people may need professional resources to aid in their coping. Resources that I cannot provide must be made available by referral. The clergy should not minimize their role even if a referral is to happen, however. Often, we may be the trusted bridge that divorced people will walk across in order to get the help they need most. On their own, they might not seek skilled professional help, but with our encouragement and vouching, they often consider new options.

There is one more outcome of the grief journey that we should acknowledge. For this, I draw from the work of Henri Nouwen. Specifically, his concept of the "Wounded Healer" is the image with which I want divorced people to connect.[21] They are not the first to suffer this disappointment and pain. They will surely not be the last. No amount of rationalization can make their divorce appear to be a good thing. However, because they are journeying through this experience, they will be dramatically altered as they move forward. Wounded though they may be, divorced people are in a unique position to help other divorced people. This is one reason support groups can work so well.

For that matter, people this wounded can potentially empathize with hurting people in other cases as well. Of course, this posture is not guaranteed for all. Empathy is not an innate trait for everyone. But our hurts change us and sometimes humble us.

Let me reemphasize that none of this is to suggest that the divorce journey was a good thing. That would be shallow and disingenuous. But since the divorce did happen, there is the possibility that the divorced person can serve as a "wounded healer" in someone else's life. That is one texture of the human experience. We can lend strength where another is weak until that person is once again strong where we are weak.

Allowing Access to Feelings

Somewhere in a mountain cabin, a middle-aged man entertains his kids. For a time, he has gotten away from his two jobs in the city. Now he does chores in his getaway place. Soon they will settle in front of a huge television to enjoy a movie. By his own confession, his thoughts occasionally stray in either of two directions. On the one hand, he is working on the details of his pending divorce terms. They are still in negotiation. Legal, financial, and custodial issues await. Decisions must be made. On the other hand, he misses his new girlfriend. Girlfriend? Already? Yes. Although she was not in his life at the time of his marital separation, his heart races when he thinks of her now. She adds excitement and acceptance to his days. Things may work out fine for him in the long haul. Only time will tell. But this quick reentry into romance worries me. Don't I want him to be happy? I want nothing more for him than happiness! So what has me concerned that he's already gone out and found a new love?

One of the scariest parts of the divorce experience seems to be figuring out what to do with all the feelings! As I write, I am scanning my personal database of memories. Some mature adults approach their divorces openly. They understand that there is work to be done, including the exploration of feelings. Much will be learned as these honest emotions are unpacked. They might seek professional counseling. They may begin a regular practice of journaling. Harnessing the power of expressed emotion, they cleanse and discover.

Over the years, I have also watched countless divorced people skillfully maneuver around their feelings. Sometimes, this sad pattern is played out with full help from trusted family and friends. The only thing worse than the attendant emotions of divorce might be admitting what those feelings really are. The notion seems to be that if one can pedal fast enough or run far enough, then those hurtful feelings can be left behind. Of course, for most the process is not as obvious as I make it seem. These people would not necessarily realize that they are harming themselves by being "busy." Getting back out there and dating seems instinctive. They might think they are in touch with their core feelings. After all, in the secrecy of home—once or twice—they have cried.

A young woman works at her job and thinks of the weekend. Less than two years prior, she was a newlywed bride! Once upon a time, family gathered and faces smiled at her wedding. Cameras clicked as the memories of a happy day were captured. Now those smiles have faded. She is in the process of getting a divorce. Some of those same family members are now whispering, as word has begun to spread that the new husband has moved out. But wait! Her social media profile indicates that there is already a significant new love in her life. Really? Yes. They are already a couple! Thus she is focused on the upcoming weekend. They are having fun. And after all, if someone brings fun into one's life, isn't that the key to a sound relationship?

Some divorced people are deflated in the face of their marital failure. Others are angry with former spouses. They are unable to function fully because this anger drives their outlooks and decisions. Still others appear numb, virtually unable to move anywhere with their lives for a time. Like boats that have become grounded, they sit and wait, but they don't know what they're waiting for.

There are many more ways one can react to this crisis. Again, dating and a new relationship seem to be instinctual responses for some divorced people. In fear, they move back out into the social waters. Afraid that age and looks will soon leave them behind, they set out to find a new love before they run out of time. Besides, everyone they listen to is cheering them on. They are encouraged to be brave enough to try again. Love will prevail, they are told. Surely a right person is out there somewhere.

While they are certainly universal in the human experience, feelings have a set of qualities that make understanding them quite elusive. Most counselors subscribe to a notion that there are a fairly small group of feelings that are basic to life. In brief, they can be described with words like happy, glad, mad, sad, and scared. While that list might sound limiting, take a closer look. Most words we would use to describe our feelings are actually derivatives of some word on this basic list. When pressed to name their feelings, some people also use words that more accurately reveal thoughts instead.

Feelings differ from thoughts. Feelings emanate from deep inside. They are not cognitive or highly processed. They capture our emotional state. While feelings may be informed by our life experiences and biases, we don't arrive at them by choice or strategy. As some people like to say, "Our feelings are neither good nor bad. They just *are!*" This captures the crucial difference between feelings and thoughts. Another view of feelings is similar: feelings are neutral; they are neither good nor bad until you act on them.

Allow me to reflect on a personal experience. When I was a child, much of my life was marked by loneliness. Other than in the confidentiality of my doctoral cohort and the occasional divorce recovery group, I have never confessed this publicly. I was an overweight child who was not readily accepted by the "cool" kids at school and church. We lived on a farm. I now look back on that setting as enriching, but at the time, my farm life was also a kind of social barrier. There were country kids and there were city kids. Much of the "in" crowd had moved from cities and lived in subdivisions. Some of we "country" kids didn't fit in.

"No problem," you might suggest. Why not just be who I was—a "farm" kid? Surely I had friends in that group? That wasn't so easy, either. The sheer acreage of the rural area we lived in also created geographic separation. While many of the kids I went to school with could simply step out their doors to be with friends on their streets, the closest people my age lived miles away. Someone who knew me in those years might be surprised to read these reflections. After all, they might point out that between school, little league, church, and my working in the family business, people constantly surrounded me. (Away from school, though, few of them were my age.) They might find the notion that I was "lonely" to be far-fetched. But consider a woman who was in my divorce group a few years ago. When she introduced herself to the group on the first night, I surprised her by naming some of her elementary school teachers. I had not seen her in at least thirty years. "We went through elementary and high school together," I said. "You and I had the same teacher several times." "I'm sorry," she said politely, "I don't remember you."

None of this is to say that I had anything other than a splendid home life. My family clearly shared love. We were actively cared for and nurtured by our parents. My brother and I were given the chance to learn and discover. I am thankful for the gift of my nuclear family that I still enjoy. In the honesty of my feelings, though, I grew up rather isolated in a crowd of people.

In midlife, I have discovered something powerful about the influence of those childhood years. With regard to feelings and thoughts, I developed an emotional pattern that still drives me today. In my relative isolation back then, I shielded myself from the pain by *thinking* first when *feeling* would have been more appropriate. As I understand things, my tendency to think through the issues of life was a way of dodging the pain I felt. When given the time away from chores or homework, I would sit and think for hours. Daydreaming and talking to myself—often speaking in monologue to my beloved dog—I had many thoughts. Still today, I at times catch myself needing the freedom to feel rather than retreating to the easy shelter of thinking.

Feelings are honest. Therein may be a large part of what makes them so scary. Depending on how we were brought up, what we believe religiously, and what values shape our lives, we may or may not have permission for some of life's feelings. We may also not have the vocabulary to express feelings if our families of origin did not often do that. If we develop enough fear of our feelings, we may begin to put up emotional shields to keep from accessing them. If we don't get around to feeling, there is less that might hurt. Thus, many divorced people embrace busyness in order to avoid their feelings. They also rush to love again.

I find that Christians struggle with anger sometimes. Many have been taught that anger is bad. While the Bible says no such thing, we have internalized the idea that there is no permission to be angry. In fact, if one is angry, we sometimes interpret a spiritual shortcoming of sorts. No genuine Christian, we are taught, should succumb to the sin of anger. Hopefully, your biblical literacy reminds you that anger is assumed. We are instructed to "sin not" in our anger (Eph 4:26). In living our daily lives, inevitably we become angry. Because this feeling is taboo, we sometimes deny our own anger, or we end up feeling conflicted because not only has something frustrating happened to us, but we also think we have sinned by getting upset. This is just one example of the forces that can drive us away from being in touch with our honest feelings.

As we expand on the basic feelings, let me mention a few common issues that divorced people face at a deep emotional level. These are evident in many participants in my divorce recovery support groups.

- *Blame.* Blame is a tricky issue. Some divorced people harbor more of the blame for the failure of their marriages than they should. The most they can be accountable for is their part of what happened. On the other extreme, many "victims" fail to search themselves for the level of blame they should own. There appears to be no such thing as a divorce where one side is completely blameless. Even in the case of alcohol or abuse, infidelity or untruth, sooner or later both parties get around to the list of things they hope not to do "next time."

- *Anger.* Anger can arise from grief. Anger can also be (rightly) directed at the ex-spouse or at oneself. It is unlikely that most people could go through something as intense as a divorce without anger. Anger can even come from unresolved guilt or blame. It finds its root in threat. Even the stigma of going through a divorce could produce anger.

- *Failure.* One's first impulse might be to tell a divorced person that he or she should never feel like a "failure." However, that is what divorced people often perceive themselves to be—failures. Among all the realities concerning a divorce, the failure of a marriage covenant is toward the top of the list. Second-guessing is an endless experience for some. We have the opportunity to help them discover that they themselves are not a failure. Their marriage was. There's a big difference.

- *Stigma.* One divorced person mentioned feeling as though she wore a "scarlet 'D'" on her forehead. Others describe feeling as though everyone is staring at them. Or they feel that even strangers they meet somehow know that they are going through a divorce. Then there is the feeling that one is the "only" divorced person in a predominantly married world. Statistics, and a quick look around, will debunk this perception. But the feeling is consistent among divorced people. Depending on one's family culture, social network, or faith background this stigma may arise from feeling that one has somehow broken several "rules" for life.

- *Self-doubt.* Having failed in a relationship as central as marriage, a person may begin to doubt her ability to function in other types of relationships. At the very least, she may doubt her ability to be an adequate romantic partner again. If a person somehow feels "stupid" because of the divorce, he could easily view himself as incompetent in other areas of life. Many divorced people come to my support group struggling with their views of themselves.

- *Trust.* Closely related to the issue of self-doubt, many divorced people express an inability to view themselves as ever trusting again. "I just don't know if I'll ever give my heart over to another person and be that vulnerable again," some of them say. They feel that if they didn't know their marriage was failing, they might once again miss the signs of further need the next time. Or if the ex-spouse was untrue, they may doubt the ability of another lover to be faithful to them in the future. Whether trust of self, or of others, this issue is acute for many who are in the pain of divorce.

- *Guilt.* A divorced person could be manipulated by an ex-spouse to own more than her fair share of guilt. But guilt can also arise from the recognition of legitimate personal fault. This kind of guilt is healthy. In either case, though, guilt is a powerful load to carry. Feeling guilt is human, but guilt is not the destination that I wish my participants to choose. I want them to travel through the guilt and then move on. Unresolved feelings of guilt can convert to anger over time.

Why does any of this matter for the divorced person? Because our feelings are where we are in life. Feelings are highly personal and are not up for negotiation by others. What we feel in a given moment might not be how we'd like to feel in life, but in that moment the feeling is an honest snapshot of a particular place in our journey. Feelings are clues to understanding. We need to attend to these markers in our journeys. When we access feelings, we have a chance to know ourselves and understand our tendencies. This kind of emotional exploration can even explain who attracts us and perhaps whom we attract. Some of the ways in which we relate work well. Other patterns do not serve us well at all. Self-awareness is the key to discovering true newness in life, but if we never take the time to learn about ourselves, we simply keep living in the same old ways.

For the two divorced people I have described in this section, what might be some of the dangers? Above, I listed heavy burdens most divorced individuals carry. Those issues must be acknowledged and dealt with constructively. Both of the people I mentioned chose the emotional shelters of "love" and busyness. On the surface, who could criticize a single father for working hard in order to provide? But consider the role those two jobs might have played in the demise of his first marriage. Less hours working might have yielded more hours at home. Many "workaholics" are actually avoiding something in their personal lives. In American culture, we are quick to applaud the initiative and the wealth that comes from such overworking without realizing how it endangers our families.

Let's stay with our hard-working dad a little longer. In our assessment, let's add the possibility that so much work might not be necessary if he weren't financially overextended (a second home with a huge television) in the first place. As for our young woman, she, too, has jumped into a brand-new relationship. There is no learning, no confrontation of self, no constructive period of aloneness. This kind of honest emotional work is not done in a day or two. The odds are that this woman has unknowingly gone out and found a virtual duplicate of the husband she is divorcing. It is just as likely that the dad has done the same. This happens often with those who do not take time to work through their relational issues and feelings. They are driven by lifelong patterns and likely relating to their new love interests in the same ways that did not work with the old ones. Feelings will wait to be processed, but they will eventually have to be faced. Emotional patterns and needs will wait to be addressed, or they will continue to drive our decisions if we do not work with them. Both of these divorced people needed alone time. They needed wise counsel and the chance to view themselves differently. What did they get instead? A new boyfriend or girlfriend. That and some good times—for a while, anyway.

Markers along the Emotional Trail: Tears, Anger, Laughter

At the start of any divorce recovery group, I try to share with my participants at least three noticeable "emotional trail markers." As participants journey through divorce, I want them to be aware of their power to self-diagnose at three major points. I credit Dr. Denise Massey of the McAfee School of Theology (Mercer University, Atlanta) with these perspectives. In her pastoral care work, she has shared these with students. Each of these noticeable happenings signals activity within and tells of progress at the feeling level. Self-awareness about these can lend us handy tools for connecting with our souls. In this brief section, I will sketch these markers as I present them in my program.

(1) *Tears.* These are an obvious occurrence. We either allow the tears to flow, in which case our eyes well up and our cheeks become wet, or we stifle the tears somehow, mumbling about something getting in our eyes. From childhood, men especially have been enculturated not to cry—certainly not when others might see them. In any event, divorced people are likely to find themselves often at the point of tears. What can we learn from tears?

When we find ourselves crying, this is *a signal that something important is happening.* That is what I want my participants to know about tears. Instead of wasting our attention on fighting them back, we should journey inward and ask ourselves what is happening that requires our attention. The nature and lessons of each important moment will be as unique as the individual, but too often we miss the clues that we could learn from if we weren't so busy fighting off the outward symptoms of the feeling.

(2) *Anger.* This is a sign that something important to us has been threatened. At first, I resisted this bit of wisdom, but upon processing and trying this signal, I have found it to be powerful. As mentioned earlier, anger is an emotion that many Christians have been discouraged from acknowledging. Unlike tears, many of us go unhindered into the angry moment. We follow the anger into actions or thoughts. When we are aware of our anger, however, we can follow it more constructively. Anger might be met with the question, *What makes me feel vulnerable right now?* As we ponder that question, we may learn more about what we are afraid of. Perhaps we might decide that the source of our anger is something that doesn't need protecting after all.

(3) *Laughter.* Genuine laughter can be a sign of adjustment. We laugh for a variety of reasons. Some people laugh and smile in order to cover their emotional trail! There is nervous laughter or inappropriate laughter. We've all heard those kinds, and have likely used them. They come at the wrong times, or they are tactics for deflecting the gravity of a given moment.

On the other hand, genuine, heart-felt laughter cleanses the soul. This release happens because the comedy of a moment penetrates the soul. That type of laughter can be triggered by a joke or by the irony of a moment. Some of life is truly funny. Unfortunately, I find that many divorced people have lost most of their ability to laugh genuinely. They may utilize the preemptive, false laughter of pain and nervousness. However, their joy and humor are harder to find. Things that might normally be funny escape their attention. They seem to have lost their permission to have fun.

The healing person is slowly rediscovering joy. She is finding the permission to laugh. She will occasionally enjoy the natural humor that life brings, or she may celebrate the escape from her pain in the company of others who just want to have fun. She may find that she can let herself go and truly enjoy those good times! Self-awareness that one is smiling and laughing—not as a cover-up but as a true release—should signal that healing is taking place. There is perspective in a discovery like this, and people should be encouraged to move forward with it.

Chapter 9

Forgiveness and Behavioral Patterns

Forgiveness: The Misguidance of the Church

Forgiveness is a key issue for most divorced people. Because of my conviction that the church has (innocently) mishandled "forgiveness" as a discipline, we have some work to do. Below, we will look at this problem as it applies to the divorced and separated. The specific people they need to forgive may vary with the circumstances, but it is rare that the issue of forgiveness does not present a struggle.

One could assume that the ex-spouse is automatically the person who most frustrates a divorced person. There is no doubt that most divorced people seem to hold their spouses to blame for a large mixture of reasons, such as the following.

- Adultery is a fairly frequent cause of marital division. In one divorce support group, 80 percent of the participants had their marriages heavily damaged by their spouses' infidelities. (By the way, let me acknowledge the obvious—infidelity is a symptom of a relationship grown weak. It is rarely the first cause of a divorce.)
- Substance abuse drives a wedge in many marriages just as powerfully as does infidelity. Marital vows or not, some partners simply reach a limit on how many times they are willing to attempt to help their spouses dry up. Eventually, leaving becomes their option of choice.
- Abuse, whether verbal or physical, is likewise a source of anger toward the ex-spouse. This issue needs little explanation.
- The death of a relationship may occur because the partners simply "quit." Not all marriages flame out. More often, in my experience, divorces

result from a slow, steady distancing. The partners eventually divest themselves of emotional commitment.

• External pressures pry some marriages apart. While the couple is still ultimately to blame, the reality is that the presenting issues often begin from outside. Job pressures, crisis in the family, financial problems, and more can bring interference into the home. Finally, one or both ex-spouses realize (too late!) that they allowed these external pressures to become primary over their commitment to each other. This is a costly lesson to learn, and usually not one that passes without some need for forgiveness of each other.

Sometimes the person who needs to be let off the hook is the person sitting in a divorce support group. Forgiveness needs can be directed inwardly. That is, some divorced people hold themselves as the target of their frustration. Ted came to the group because he had alienated his spouse. Through some noticeable gaps in his emotional intelligence, he had slowly pushed away the woman who had once loved him. Only in retrospect did he see his own personality issues as the key divider. The need to forgive himself, and to learn from his mistakes, was paramount in his mind.

The session in which we deal with the topic of forgiveness is usually a powerful one, but it is also tough. I find that many of my group members have to process this issue for some time before the benefit fully manifests. Others connect readily with what we discuss. Most of my participants need, and want, some guidance on forgiveness.

What has the church done to hamper personal understandings of forgiveness? Through good intent, we have represented the transaction of forgiveness as having some characteristics that it cannot live up to. The Bible leaves us with a clear impression that forgiveness must happen. Matthew 6:9-15 offers no less than what we refer to as "The Lord's Prayer." At the close of this passage we read, "For if you forgive men when they sin against you, your heavenly Father will also forgive you. But if you do not forgive men their sins, your Father will not forgive your sins." None of us want to run afoul of the opportunity to be cleansed by God for our transgressions. There is urgency, and profound theological wisdom, to the biblical instructions on this issue. We know we should forgive.

Think back to when you were a child. Your friend came over to play, and you did something you weren't supposed to do. The other child's crying brought your parents in to investigate. Soon, they were leading you by the hand until you were face to face with your (upset) friend. "Tell him you're sorry!" your parents said. Through gritted teeth, you said, "I'm sorry." You might not have meant it, but you said it. Later that day, when your friend's parents were apprised of the argument, they might have led your friend back over to you. "Tell him you forgive him!" Thus, we begin to learn that apology and forgiveness are handled ceremonially and instantly. The church has taken the sacred teachings and enculturated their implications to a level that is disconnected with life. We have strived to make forgiveness sound not only important but also doable. In our unction to do as God has instructed, perhaps we trivialize the tough work that needs to be done regarding forgiveness.

What is forgiveness probably *not* going to be in our lives? Let's take a closer look so that we can help divorce recovery participants as they struggle with this issue. Forgiveness is not necessarily

• *a quick transaction.* Again, the church rightly teaches the biblical notion that we should forgive and seek forgiveness. Like the flip of a light switch, we think we should transact forgiveness and apology. In fact, much guilt can come when one realizes that the heart simply has not caught up with the head or the soul. This is particularly confusing if one truly wishes to move on but cannot. No matter the intentions, the true feelings involved in forgiveness have to get on board. Eventually, forgiveness is a choice, but even that decision is not the emotional finish line.

• *a public act.* Forgiveness may involve words and intentions and even ceremony. The 1990s could rightly be nicknamed "The Decade of the Apology." Groups voted on and issued resolutions that apologized for deeds committed years and even centuries before, but the reality of individual forgiveness takes place much more privately. Also, the conscious state of having forgiven is usually noticed much more retrospectively.

• *only a spiritual issue.* When the relationship is important enough and the circumstances damaging enough, forgiveness can take a long time. We may be theologically convicted about our need to forgive or to apologize. Still, these motivators may not prevail immediately.

• *a path to reconciliation.* Some relationships need to go their separate ways. Forgiving someone need not obligate a person to resume as though nothing had happened. In fact, forgiveness may be merely a stop along the path to final closure, as the relationship is over for good.

• *an indicator that the matter will be forgotten.* Forgiving someone does not obligate us to act as though the transgression never happened. We attribute to God the ability to both "forgive and forget." We count on the belief that, in Christ, our forgiven sins are removed from God ". . . as far as the East is from the West" (Ps 103:12). Humans do not necessarily possess this capacity. We may think we should, but life will throw us irreconcilable problems.

In the late 1980s, someone central to my life hurt me deeply. At the time, we talked openly in apology and forgiveness. In fact, the misdeed had taken place earlier over a period of years. This had to be resolved, so we finally made vows to move on. These words reflected our sincere intentions. We even had one conversation that was ceremonial enough that I can still picture the setting and remember the words. We meant what we said. I still trust to this day that the other person was as sincere in their words as I was in accepting and "granting" them forgiveness. But I became conflicted when I realized some time later that the hurt and frustration were still with me. A year passed. I was still hurt.

Still a few more years passed, and I could not forget. I began to doubt my spiritual personhood. My fitness to be a minister became a new struggle for me because I could not believe my own inability to grant true forgiveness. I was enslaved by the hurt and now the guilt. The relationship continued. We saw each other regularly. Finally, some thirteen years later, I was with that person one random day, and I realized without a doubt that I had forgiven them. To this day, that forgiveness has enriched our bond, but there was no magic moment that I could put my finger on as to when the change came about. It simply did somewhere along the journey.

Ironically, we Christians need to make peace with forgiveness and apology. Eventually, we must let go of our idealized visions of these issues. We need to allow life's realities to be informed by our faith, but we must also adopt realistic hopes. When we do, we are able to walk the journey freed of expectations that are bound to let us down.

I have been candid about what I believe forgiveness not to be. Now it is time for me to explain what I think forgiveness is. Consider the following:

- *Apology and forgiveness lend an opportunity for expression.* There is a power in hearing aloud what has heretofore existed in one's heart. Whether or not there is reconciliation, this expression renders each person the chance to let out what they have been filtering through internally.
- *Forgiveness can bring clarity.* Both parties have a better chance of knowing each other's motivations and reasons. Perhaps closure and fracture will be the end results, but at least the guesswork can be removed. Ideally, a sense of understanding happens—perhaps even understanding that facilitates healing.

- *Forgiveness is a choice.* Sometimes we have to do what we do not feel like doing. Forgiveness comes from both the heart and the head.
- *Forgiveness is a journey and a process.* One person has said, "We forgive in pieces." (I tried my best to find attribution for that quote, but failed.) That captures the complex, extended nature of forgiveness. It takes a day of healing here and a moment of perspective there. It takes one new experience with the person who has hurt us, and eventually we feel differently toward him or her. Indeed, we forgive in pieces.
- *Forgiveness makes us vulnerable.* The apology may or may not be accepted. We might appear to be taken advantage of by not holding the grudge. The other party might not prove to be sincere in their part of the bargain. We hand over a little of ourselves in the deal. There is risk, but if there is to be a tomorrow for any meaningful relationship, then this level of vulnerability must be extended now and then.
- *Forgiveness can lead to renegotiation of the terms of the relationship.* People have the chance to define the terms of their relationship moving forward. Often, this happens in tandem with a conversation in which forgiveness seems to be the primary subject. If we teach others how to treat us, then this renegotiation is often where boundaries and terms are exchanged.
- *We learn through forgiveness.* If we had a choice, we would likely want to do without the pain and the circumstances that caused it. However, we cannot change the fact that the episode happened. The breach is real, but we are left different because of the experience. We hope to store the lessons of the episode so that we do not repeat the same mistakes.

Breaking Free of Powerful Relationship Patterns

We think that when we grow up, we are our "own" people, but we sit in the office doing things the way we did them at home when an older sibling was ordering us around. Or we say something one of our parents would have said and then wonder, "Where did that come from?" Beginning at surprisingly early ages, we are formed by the roles we play in our families of origin. Some people even theorize that the imprint of how our parents act out their marital/parental roles determines how we enact those same roles in adulthood. It even affects what draws us to other people.

As adults, we naturally recoil at the notion that we are not in charge of such big issues as our thoughts, attractions, and feelings. Are we hopelessly locked into our roles and images? Of course not. But realizing the driving influences in our lives is a key to self-awareness, and self-awareness is the beginning of being intentional about how we relate to our partners. An event like a divorce gives us a natural reason to examine these emotional realities.

Being late for baseball practice or church for the umpteenth time pushed me to embarrassment as a child. It frustrated me. This is a favorite example I use. From middle-school age on, I generally swore that "someday" I wouldn't be late everywhere I went. Guess what? A good schedule is like a security blanket to me now. As kids, we start listing things we will do differently from the way our parents did them. Some of those things will fall off the list as we get older and our parents suddenly get smarter. We are not as aware of other patterns and biases. We simply live by them. Conscious or not, we do intentionally leave some of these behind as we chart our own relational courses. Even the behaviors we take on because of something we want to leave behind are actually shaped by our families of origin. Though you are now an independent adult, your parents and siblings are still shaping you in some ways. Again, this is an honest and helpful bit of knowledge to have.

There is a field of couples' work that has emerged somewhat recently. Imago Relationship Therapy came about in part from the book *Getting the Love You Want* by Harville Hendrix.[22] This framework helps me understand the couples in my support groups and the work of divorce. The patterns in which we relate to others become more workable. Basic to this is the notion that we emerge from our families of origin with certain *imago* or "images of roles." These images are formed earlier than most of us might believe. They capture what we know of how one carries out the role of wife, mother, husband, father, brother or sister, and son or daughter. To be certain, we reach independent adulthood, and we are considered fully responsible for our own decisions, actions, and words.

Within that responsible reality, though, we tend to do things the way we're used to doing them. When we choose people for the roles of our adult lives, our choices are informed somewhat by what we have brought forward—or left behind—from the family of origin. That is, we choose (consciously and mostly unconsciously) who will best fit with the way we know how to live. We might not be aware that a partner reminds us somehow of our mother or father. We might not know that our spouse fits naturally with our understanding of how to "room" with our brothers and sisters. In reality, there are some dimensions of our romantic relationships that are shaped by these role images. You'll hear it when a friend or participant tells about their serious love: "Even on our first date, it seemed like we had known each other forever!" "I just can't describe how natural our relationship feels. So free and easy."

Even what we've decided to do differently is shaped to a degree by our home images: what we like, what we dislike; our habits about house cleaning, schedules, traditions, biases; and even our attraction to the person we seek to love and the other person's attraction to us. There are powerful old forces at play. Beyond that, we also bring with us certain patterns of relating. What might these patterns be like? Consider these behaviors:

• An attack from someone else might cause you to retreat because that's what it took to survive in your family of origin. You tend to withdraw from others when things get intense.

• You don't need to be the CEO of your company because you were a younger sibling among a few kids in your family. You were way down the pecking order. As an adult, you can contribute and be creative, but you don't have to be in charge of the world because that's never been an option or even an agenda for you.

• Your parents were heavy handed and didn't allow the flexibility of discussion where decisions—or discipline—were concerned. Pushing back wasn't rewarded where you grew up. As an adult, you might attack loudly and even aggressively if confronted. Somewhere along the way, you promised you would stand up for yourself once you left home. Now you attack when provoked.

• Maybe you were lonely as a child. Although you had many feelings that you needed to process, there was mostly no one around to listen to you. Along the way, you directed these feelings inward. You might have learned to deny them, or you might have developed a pattern of processing them as thoughts. In adulthood, you now tend to deflect your feelings into thoughts. On the other hand, you might have been made to work, and often your lonely emotional journey was worked out in chores or events.

I attended a "going away" party recently. A family was sending out their child following his college graduation. He would soon be working and frequently on the road. I asked the father how they were dealing with this big change. He immediately pointed to his wife and said, "She copes by throwing a party." I thought his words were insightful. He was aware that his wife was not so much celebrating as she was busily distracting herself—and commemorating the passage. What the father may not have seen is that when I asked him a "you all" question, he deflected his own coping by telling me about his wife's. She gets busy and throws a party! He . . . well, I still don't know. But he deflects. That I do know.

Any of these patterns might be understood more as you reflect upon how you did things in your family of origin. These patterns can also be understood as *adaptive behaviors*. They are emotional reactions we developed along the way in response to not getting something we wanted or needed from others. The few examples above are simply ways to illustrate one of the shaping forces that emerge with us into adulthood. Some of these patterns work well in relationships. Others of them do not. A second- or third-time divorced person will often berate herself because she has caught on to some of the relational traps she seems to fall into repeatedly. Some people refer to these troublesome adaptive behaviors as *maladaptive behaviors*. In a divorce, these latter patterns need particular attention. A person may require the help of a counselor in order to develop awareness of their patterns, much less to interrupt those that need to be altered.

Divorces don't often arise from single incidents. Your scary argument will rarely end a marriage unless it turns physically violent. Much more likely, a divorce results from repeated issues. The emotional goodwill of a couple becomes depleted by patterns of relating that simply do not work. Rather than adding emotional capital to the accounts, they instead burn these reserves with conflict or dysfunction.

What can we do with all of this? In a next relationship, divorced people want to continue using the parts of who they are that work, but they need to have learned about their own tendencies, especially the patterns that seem to lead down unproductive or hurtful paths. A next love deserves a more aware partner. Some of this insight could be gained by a personal journey inward, but much of this will come to light over time in the context of a support group discussion. It is even more likely to become clear after some good work with a skilled counselor. Being scared of what one might discover is an understandable fear. Skipping the opportunity to learn about oneself, though, is not the best course. Evaluating readiness for a next relationship requires better self-awareness. Evaluating the relative health of a next relationship will also benefit when a person knows himself or herself better, and that is the goal of divorce recovery support.

Section III
Divorce Recovery File Folder

Introduction to Divorce and Marriage Helps

What started as a gap-filling resource for my work has become a set of pages I hope will be helpful. Like you, I had access to books, articles, and helpful web sites galore! They are the real backbone of my resources. Still, something was missing. I needed a piece to hand to people that would sketch out basic thoughts in a quick, non-threatening fashion. For those of you who work with pre-marital, married, or divorcing people, you now have Marriage Helps and Divorce Helps. These quick, two-page guides started as a way to overview key life issues with my couples and divorced individuals. Because I work with a high volume of people in each life stage, I found a need for something that human beings would actually read!

Indeed, each of these topics could comprise an expansive book or a web site unto itself, but I find that on introduction, people aren't going to sit down and give a high level of focus to a topic unless they are guided into it. That's what these resources do. They act almost like a relational "mirror" that my marriage and divorce participants can hold up in front of themselves. They are written conversationally in an attempt to connect and inspire. Often, these pages help start dialogue in the next session after people have read them. The participant comes back in and references a key thought from one of these topics and wants to talk more about it. Then we have something to work with! Remember that the best resource is the one that will actually be used!

Surprisingly, my Divorce Recovery participants have requested the Marriage Helps pages to the extent that we've also begun to bind these into the resource book we hand out to those entering each group. To be honest, the utility of the marriage pieces is rather forensic in nature. The notion is that people want to read them as a "mirror" to look into retrospectively, as well as to anticipate being in healthier relationships again one day. I celebrate that!

I hope you'll find these resources to be a bridge you can use to invite your participants in for deeper exploration.

Divorce Helps

Eight Questions Divorced People Often Ask

1. I feel like such a failure. What does this say about me?
Let's not insult you by diminishing the seriousness of your divorce. That wouldn't be a helpful starting place. But let's *do* cut to the chase: you have suffered the death of a central relationship in your life. A lasting commitment fell short. Despite your best wishes, you and your spouse could not work out your shortcomings. However, let's focus on the question. What does this say about *you*? It says exactly what we've already expressed in this paragraph. This divorce suggests that you have a lot of work to do. You must renew your self-awareness. What the divorce does not say is that *you* are a failure. In proper context, your marriage was a large and important part of who you are, but it was never all of who you are. Learn from the terrible experience. Work toward healthier understandings of how to relate. Above all, know that this chapter isn't your final word!

2. If everything happens for a reason, what is God's reason for my divorce?
This way of believing is popular these days. If the celebrities on *Entertainment Tonight* are your best substitute for theologians, then it at least sounds cool to hear them say that everything happens for a reason. The trouble is that this belief doesn't square with any theology I've ever taught or preached. You'll find it a flimsy idea to stand on during your crisis. Sooner or later, you're going to get around to asking, "Why would a loving God do this (or cause this, or allow this) just to teach me something?" The Bible makes a case not only that God isn't the author of evil but also that God isn't capable of causing evil or pain. Much of the time, human causes are more at the center of our difficulty than cosmic or spiritual ones. The better question might be, "Where will God *be* in my divorce experience?"

3. How will I get the confidence to love again?
For your unique life, this question is a journey that will take some time. I remain convinced that some of the healing is accomplished by getting reacquainted with yourself. Learn about what went wrong, on both sides, in your marriage. Learn about what really matters in life and about what is important for you to have/give in a loving relationship. Figure out some of what makes a "healthy" relationship and what is unhealthy. I'm also convinced that in focusing on strengthening your non-romantic relationships, such as the ones you have with friends, family, and coworkers, you learn more about love.

4. Is it just me, or is everybody staring at me?
No, everybody is not likely staring at you. But the change in your life makes you feel as though you're under incredible scrutiny. Let's be candid: most people don't *know* you're divorced or separated. Fewer still actually care, if we're honest. You are feeling some of your own self-focus in the moment. That's not all bad. You are also feeling distance because key family and friends don't know exactly how to relate to you in this painful time. Social alliances have been altered. The way out is the way through. Keep loving yourself, keep loving others, and keep giving the people in your life permission to love you too. I think you'll find that the spotlight will dim soon.

5. Isn't God mad at us? I've heard that the Bible says God "hates" divorce.
In my ministry, I find that there are those who don't want the church to talk about "sin." There are also those who acknowledge wrong but insist that the church should only talk about God's grace. Let's admit that God clearly hates divorce. When you sealed your vows, divorce was not the desired outcome. But staying in a dangerous or harmful relationship isn't God's intent for you either. I am confident that God hurts *with* you. I am confident that God *forgives* shortcomings when asked genuinely. I am confident that God wants you to move forward in life, renewed and matured. Lastly, I am confident that God is not mad at you. Confess. Cleanse. Ask forgiveness. Grow!

6. Sometimes the pain is so intense that I feel like there has been a death in my family. Is there hope for me?
There *has* been a death in your family. Your greatest marital hopes, dreams, and commitments have passed away. The love you shared let you down, and the partner you dreamed of is no longer your married partner. The grief of

divorce is painfully real. It will not simply fade with time. Be fair to yourself, and do not diminish the importance of the pain.

7. What would a healthy relationship look like? How would I know if I were in one?
- Healthy relationships center on acceptance and understanding.
- Each of you is free to express, to think, and to do as you are gifted.
- You know where each other's "buttons" are but care too much to push them!
- You can work together, problem-solve together, and dream together.
- You want the best for your partner as much as or even more than you do for yourself.
- You share a common purpose.
- You are loved actively and noticeably.
- You can trust and depend on your partner.

8. At this age, won't I be lonely the rest of my life? My clock's ticking!
Again, your journey is *your* journey. For some, the fear of being alone could not be any less a concern. For others, this is a real fear. Let me remind you of two things. First, you have proven once that you could get yourself married. You can probably do it again. Second, why not free yourself from letting that urgency drive you more than it should? Rather than fear, why not be guided by getting to know yourself all over again? Maybe you can learn how to invest in significant relationships that already exist in your life. It sounds like a gamble, but give yourself some time free of the distractions of a serious relationship. Rediscover the "you" that you'll want to offer someone in the future.

Seven Myths about Your Divorce Experience

1. I should just get back on the horse and ride again.
This is one of the first pieces of advice your friends and family may give. Of course, they mean well. In some cases, they may have even picked out the next person for you to love! The problem is that this approach doesn't fix anything. Falling quickly back into "love" only distracts you from the pain, and it heightens the chances that you will repeat the same relational patterns with a person who is similar to your ex-spouse. Instead, it is best to take time to determine what happened to your first marriage and learn from it; take a

minimum of one lap around the calendar after your divorce experience, and take another lap once you find yourself in a new love.

2. *Everything happens for a reason (as if God caused the divorce).*
This way of believing is popular these days. If the celebrities on *Entertainment Tonight* are your best substitute for theologians, then it at least sounds cool to hear them say that everything happens for a reason. The trouble is that this belief doesn't square with any theology I've ever taught or preached. You'll find it a flimsy idea to stand on during your crisis. Sooner or later, you're going to get around to asking, "Why would a loving God do this (or cause this, or allow this) just to teach me something?" The Bible makes a case not only that God isn't the author of evil but also that God isn't capable of causing evil or pain. Much of the time, human causes are more at the center of our difficulty than cosmic or spiritual ones. The better question might be, "Where will God *be* in my divorce experience?" Of course, I can't make you believe as I do about this theological matter, but I at least want to raise the question for you. Wrestle with it, and come to your own conclusions.

3. *Having gone through a divorce once, I won't make the same mistake again.*
Unfortunately, this is a myth because most people actually do make the mistake again if they fail to do the emotional work required to recover from a first divorce. We all live out certain patterns of behavior. Some of these patterns work better for us than others do, and the maladaptive patterns need to be interrupted. In order to have a healthier relationship next time, one must take the time to heal and learn. "How much time?" you ask. It varies from person to person depending on their particular issues and at what pace they make the discoveries/learn the lessons that reshape what drives their way of loving. Simply having experienced something once doesn't mean it won't happen again. If we learned that quickly and easily, none of us would have the repeated stories of how we didn't seem to learn our lesson the first time.

4. *I'm not sure I can ever trust or love again.*
It can happen, but for many divorced people, the will to love again takes time. Some hit the dating scene like they're on a mission to "get out there" and do it right this time. Others would say, "I'm personally interested in more certainty because I never want to go through this again." The bottom line is that there are no guarantees, but if you do what one lawyer participant termed "extensive due diligence," you'll stand a better chance. That means

there are no shortcuts to the vulnerable, risky emotional exploration that *every* person who has gone through a divorce needs to do. Ask yourself these questions:

• How did this happen?
• What was my part of the blame in the whole scenario? (This question often seems preposterous to most participants, and this issue alone can take months to surface after divorce!)
• What patterns of relating do I bring to the table that may need attention?
• What help do I need in order to do the work of "recovery"?
• What will my version of recovery be?
• What would a healthy relationship look like (sound like, feel like) if I were in one?

5. *Time heals all wounds. If I can stay busy enough, I will heal.*
This mindset is instinctive and almost always destructive. Among other things, your divorce experience is a loss. Divorce grief closely approximates the grief of human death in our lives. You must deal with it and work on healing. You must move toward growth that is only possible as you deal with the grief. You will need to spend enough time to unplug and reflect. That's not easy in our culture of noise, speed, and distraction, but your grieving will wait on you! There is no such thing as healthfully "busying" your way through something while you heal. If you defer your grief, it will still be there years later. Name it, work on it, and grow through it.

6. *I'm the exception to the norm. I learned my lessons while my experience was happening.*
Actually, you are probably not the exception you think you are. You probably weren't learning as you went through the divorce. Others around you were, but probably not you. We tell ourselves that we are strong, or our friends and family tell us we are smart and different. Convincing yourself that you are exceptional is more likely a defense born of denial. Take an honest look at yourself and see if you are truly ready to move on without a time of support and hard emotional work. Most likely, you are not.

7. *I don't have the time or the emotional energy to do the hard work I need to do. I'm a busy person.*
You do have the time. We do what we decide is important to do. You must do this work so that you can move forward with your life. If you have the

baggage of this experience hanging around and waiting to be unpacked, it will hold you back. On the other hand, learning and growing will make you a better person. If you do the necessary work, you'll move forward to more possibility in life, including the possibility of healthy and enjoyable relationships of all kinds. Remember, if you don't work through the issues now, they will wait on you.

Qualities of a Healthy Relationship

1. *Your partner "gets" you and you "get" your partner.*
I have to be careful with this point. Someone could interpret this in a self-absorbed way and think it means they can act any way they please, and that their partner should just "get" it. That's not the idea. Instead, in a healthy love relationship, we know when someone understands and connects with us. We should be able to sense when they don't. When someone doesn't "get" you, they may never "get" you. Why would you delve into a serious relationship with someone with whom you probably aren't going to connect? Desperation, expediency, fear, pressure—these can all drive us to overlook the obvious. We can sense that something isn't right, but then deny that there is a problem. When it's right, it's right. When it's not, it's time to make a decision.

2. *You share at least six key intimacies.*
There are key elements in a healthy relationship. In fact, marriage enrichment leaders Otis and Deigie Andrews suggest there are six "intimacies" necessary for a healthy relationship.[23] Sexual intimacy may come to mind first. Beyond that, though, there is work intimacy. Managing a house and a family is hard work. Some couples can work together; others can't. Intellectual intimacy suggests that you don't always agree, but that you respect and accept each other's thoughts. Spiritual intimacy, crisis intimacy, and emotional intimacy round out the set. I speak to these in more detail in a separate article. These are basic tasks and connections in life. When one or more of them is weak (or missing), there is work to be done. With help, you can strengthen these.

3. *Healthy communication is a regular practice (and a relational enrichment tool).*
Some couples allow their communication practices to fade. Others never quite develop them as helpfully as they should. In a relationship that works,

a couple wants to communicate with each other, and not only for pragmatic reasons. They want to hear what is on each other's minds. They want to be sure they understand each other and can diffuse their conflicts as smoothly as possible. They won't always agree with each other, and they surely won't always like to hear what is said. No two partners can be on the same page all the time, but communication is worth the work. It is worth negotiating, including the boundaries within which arguments can be waged. Oh, and healthy couples know how to communicate their love, too!

4. *Conflict resolution happens within bounds and is valued above winning.*
There are "boundaries" for arguing. We call this "fighting fair." Somewhere along the way, a a healthy couple negotiates the border between what they can say to each other in anger, and what they can't. They also establish a rhythm and a pace for dealing with conflict. One may want to talk it all out now, but the other needs space for a while. Eventually, they meet in the middle. A healthy couple also understands that "winning" isn't winning if the relationship emerges damaged. In a relationship that works, conflict will happen. But the commitment and love that drive resolution eventually take over. A solution that honors both parties is the one that is chosen. Few topics of argument are worth the destruction of the relationship. No two partners can think alike, or work so alike, as to avoid conflict. A healthy pair figures out a way to keep differences from turning toxic. Unhealthy couples simply begin fighting.

5. *You feel accepted, valued, and safe with your partner.*
While it is unthinkable to some, there are people who are committed to relationships they know are not working. Perhaps you've been there. But in a next partner, you are looking to see if you are accepted. Is your partner constantly trying to reshape you? We all could use tweaking, but when a relationship is focused on the attempt to change each other, both parties might need to reevaluate. In a healthy partnership, each person values the other. You are equal, and you are important to each other. Your relationship is not a side hobby when there is nothing else to do. Also, in a healthy relationship you trust your partner. You are safe with that person—physically, emotionally, and otherwise. Can't trust your partner? You aren't trustworthy yourself? This is either an issue you need to work on, or you must ask yourself if you can live without it.

6. Your partner challenges you to be a better person, but not through criticism.
Does your partner bring out the best in you? That's a healthy quality. We can all learn from each other. But there is a moral and ethical component that feeds off a healthy partnership. When we are the presence of Christ to each other, we cannot help but grow. There are surely things your partner will do more naturally than you do them, and vice versa. Hopefully, the best of who we are rubs off on each other. In small ways, we reshape each other a bit in a good relationship.

7. You know where each other's "buttons" are, but you love each other too much to push them.
This one is rather simple, yet too many of us have been in relationships in which both partners did the opposite. We don't have to be with someone for long to figure out what makes the person angry. Soon, we learn how far we can push each other and cause damage. Or we provoke each other to act out in ways that aren't productive. We know how to hurt each other. The thing about a healthy partnership is that when you love and value each other, you don't want to cause hurt. You don't want to bring out bad habits and behaviors. There's no victory in provocation.

8. You can work together and solve problems creatively.
Life brings challenges. While you won't respond to each challenge perfectly, a healthy relationship works over the stretch of time. In a healthy relationship, you can eventually work together freely and creatively to arrive at a solution. In unhealthy relationships, partners react to challenges with rivalry or conflict. Rather than ending up with a fulfilling victory, conflicted couples simply find a new topic over which to compete.

9. Did we mention "fun" yet?
"Fun" sounds childish. This is too bad since some hurting people can't remember the last time they truly enjoyed being with their partner. Long ago, the relationship grew lonely and drab. Maybe the toxicity got so pronounced that the notion of fun was laughable. Of course, you want to have more in common than fun. But in a healthy relationship, you want to see your love walk in the door. You have things you enjoy doing together. Your partner can put a smile on your face, and does so regularly!

Key Attitudes of Divorce Recovery

Some attitudes hold significant power for healing. They'll serve you well. Their opposites will weigh you down and hurt you. An *antonym* is a word expressing an opposite meaning. Fast is the antonym of slow. There is healing power in the attitudes we choose for life. There is a fake-it-until-you-make-it component to divorce recovery. Sometimes in life, we have to choose what we want to be. Then we have to live that way until we reach the point of being able to own that stance. Below, we'll explore some attitudinal choices that carry tremendous healing power, and we'll also note their antonyms. When we are living these opposites, we'll pay their destructive costs.

1. *Have some genuine* goodwill *toward your friends and family.*
This seems obvious, but our pain can rob us of our ability to be happy even for those we love most. During your unhappiness, your friends and loved ones will still achieve. Good things will happen to them while you are still feeling devastated. They will experience good fortune while you think nothing good is ever coming your way again. *Envy* is a destructive force. It can make you angry about others' happiness. Instead, you could choose to be genuinely happy for those you love. Why should they go without your support during your difficult recovery chapter? Oddly, the capacity to be happy for others is likely to spark new health for you. Goodwill could be one trail that leads you toward a different perspective about life.

2. *People who overcome terrible disappointment share a trait: they can sit in the ashes and* envision *their first steps toward a new chapter.*
That's not an original thought. I wish it were. Actually, in a Harvard Business School publication, authors Warren Bennis and Robert Thomas explored this trait.[24] Life knocks us all down. Relationships fail, and so do companies. Those more likely to rebound and thrive are those who find a new plan. Even in the midst of the hurt, they have a vision. Goals, action steps, or even instinctual senses of direction are freed to form the next chapter of life! People with this attitude can at least see that there is something better out there. They allow themselves to dream and to plan. They go to work learning from the disappointment so that they can eventually move toward the next chapter. The opposite is *tunnel vision*—the sense that your current hurt is all there will be to life from now on. Vision springs from a conviction that it's time to move forward.

3. *The stance of a* wounded healer *will lead you to heal by the sharing of yourself.*
You didn't choose to be wounded, but you can choose to help others through similar circumstances. An antonym for wounded healer might be *paralyzed*. I'm not sure I would try to convince you that helping others will eventually make your pain seem worthwhile. For some of you, that might prove to be true. For many of you, it won't. I do know this: your lot in life as a divorce survivor is your new reality. That's not fair, but it does make you uniquely postured to lend help to others around you. Jack Lemmon, the actor, left behind this thought: "I've found that when you have risen in life, you are obligated to send the elevator back down so it can lift others, too." He's right. Your pain and experience could make you the person someone else draws from in their divorce recovery. Wounded? Yes. Healer? That, too. The writer Henri Nouwen explored this concept and made us aware that from our brokenness (we all have some broken places), we can reach out. In doing so, we will discover a new perspective, fresh strength, and more helpful power.

4. *The* willingness *to choose healthful attitudes is an attitude itself.*
Some right attitudes or actions in life still have to be chosen. Even in Christianity, sometimes the "will" to do what is right has to be learned. We have to choose it. When we are hurt, we often lose touch with that willingness. As if life owes us a break, we feel that we should be able to marinate in our misery. One antonym of willing is *unwilling*. Others include *unable* or *disinclined*. Some things that matter simply must be chosen. If we wait until we feel ready to live healthfully among other people, the world may be on hold for a while! Choosing to go in a helpful direction may lead us back to a healthier way eventually.

5. *You will need to draw deeply from* hope.
I wish there were a pill you could take that would replenish a sense of hope. If there were, I would get out a prescription pad and write one up for you. But there isn't. Let's think our way toward an attitude of hope. By the way, what's the opposite of hope? *Despair* is one word. Perhaps you think hope isn't anywhere to be found. But despair probably isn't what you want either. Look around you. You aren't the first divorced person you've known. Take out a piece of paper and jot down four names of divorced people who have eventually moved on to happier chapters of their lives. Focus on them. Interview them if you are willing. Listen to how they got to that point. Draw from their examples of hope. Believe that there is something else out there.

You may learn what their journeys were like. Expose yourself to living realities of hope until that attitude becomes a part of who you are again.

6. *A curiosity about life will enrich and guide you.*
Divorce robbed you of some childlikeness—that is, if any of yours was still intact by the time your divorce or separation occured. Those who endured years of brokenness in their marriages especially paid a price. Your life can bring you to a point where everything in sight appears serious. In the midst of all that seriousness, we need to play. Oddly, those who renew their spirits—and their resources—often follow a sense of curiosity. Are you thinking about trying something new? Explore that possibility. Are you wondering about a subject that is new? Read about it. Are you not sure what something is? Look into it. No one gets to set your life curriculum except you! The antonym for curious is *uninquisitive*. That's not where I want to be in life. How boring would that be?

Wrestling with Forgiveness Issues

A MESSY ISSUE
When your friends and family are helping you distract yourself through a divorce, "forgiveness" is not an appealing pastime. Compared with watching television, going out, or even doing your taxes, working at forgiveness is not fun. Though we may try, issuing a simple statement like "I forgive and I am done with it!" won't do the job. Sooner or later, we have to decide who may need our forgiveness. We need to identify what we need to forgive. We evaluate what such forgiveness will cost us emotionally, and what difference reaching that state of forgiveness will make. These aren't quick decisions if the hurt is deep enough. Eventually, we have to reach a point of readiness. Sometimes that arrives later even than our resolve to forgive.

A STATE OF BEING
Forgiveness on a particular issue may turn out to be a state of being. That is, we may first reach a rational or spiritual conclusion that forgiveness is needed. Lagging slightly behind may be the arrival at a point where we know that we have indeed forgiven. Our parents took us by the hand and made us hear the apology of a sibling or the kid down the street. Through clenched teeth, we mouthed the words, "I forgive," so that we would comply with their orders. But we walked away knowing we didn't mean what we said. The

same thing happens to us as adults. We can feel the need to forgive, but arriving at true forgiveness reaches beyond our intent.

A Prison that Holds Us Captive

What's at stake? Why does this really matter? Unresolved forgiveness issues can hold us hostage in life. Carrying around so much anger, pain, confusion, or regret holds us back. When the problem is big enough, we play and replay what happened. This takes focus and energy from other things we might need to do. Whether you need to grant the forgiveness or ask for it, these issues have power. Part of the process is in reaching the point where you are tired of paying the price that the issue exacts from you. Once you reach this point, sorting through some of the other parts of the equation may seem reasonable. You may feel that your stance is righteous, but holding on to the pain is costly!

A Misunderstood Religious Act

I tell divorced people that the church has done culture a disservice. In our zeal to (rightly) emphasize the moral imperative—or psychological health—of forgiveness, we may pay another price. We can add guilt to life. We can make ourselves feel as though something is wrong with us because we didn't quickly and easily let something go. That is, the church has made forgiveness sound like an act that can happen in an instant. Depending on our personal makeup and the circumstances involved, the process can actually become quite drawn out. Here's the reality: one person has said, "We forgive in pieces." Church and culture make forgiveness sound like a simple decision. From there, we assume our resolve should take care of the problem immediately. Instead, resolve may only be the beginning of the forgiveness journey. A particularly pious believer might say, "But that's all wrong. We forgive and we leave it behind. Just like God does." Unfortunately, neither you nor I are God. We cannot relate to what should be. We can only live in the reality we have. The messy fact is that we can't always speed up the emotional process simply by wanting to forgive someone badly enough. Nor can we make it happen by feeling convicted that we should forgive.

More than a Sentiment or a Resolve

The process of forgiveness is complicated because our intent is only part of the battle. No matter our sentiment, no matter our resolve, forgiveness takes time, especially if the person or the issue involved matters to you. Life can be confusing when we realize that our genuine intent is to forgive, and yet we simply aren't yet at that point. We confuse our words or our decision to forgive with the act of forgiving. I remember once telling a loved one that I forgave them. I meant those words sincerely. We had a long, drawn-out conversation. I wanted to move on. But arriving at a place where I knew I had truly forgiven the person took years after our initial conversation.

Sometimes Unexpected and Surprising
Let's pursue that last story further. Now and then, I would ask myself what was wrong. Why had I not been able to let the issue go? Those years passed, and at various checkpoints I reviewed where I seemed to be. Then, one day, I thought of the person. I thought of the hurt. I thought of the issues involved. And I knew that I had arrived at forgiveness. The funny thing is that I couldn't identify exactly when this had happened. There was no *aha* moment I could recall. Nothing seemed to have changed, except that I knew I was now on the other side of forgiveness. I could see in life's rear-view mirror that my resolve, and my words, had now been matched by reality. Since then, that clarity has been born out. The relationship, and me personally, are both in better places because I was truly able to forgive.

A Two-way Street
So far, this discussion has been about your need to offer forgiveness. However, you may be the one who needs forgiveness. Perhaps either you or your ex-spouse need to consider forgiving *you*! One of the toughest struggles in our divorce recovery groups is the night we consider both parties' mixture of blame for the dissolution of their marriages. Some are at a point where they are ready to consider their own contribution to the divorce. Others, though, see themselves as blameless victims. Usually, they are focused only on the abuse, infidelity, or pain their ex-spouse caused. They cannot consider the ways in which they, too, failed to be the perfect spouse. In any divorce, there is blame to spread both ways. One act some leaders recommend is asking your ex-spouse to forgive you. Caution: this request may go unanswered or be responded to in a way that further hurts. When you ask your ex for forgiveness, you'd better not hang your hopes on any specific answer you'd like in return. The act of making the request may be more important to your healing than the response you get.

A Word about What Forgiveness Is Not
Forgiving isn't acting as though the hurt never happened. Forgiving isn't an obligation to reconcile the relationship. Nor is it an injustice to the one who

was hurt. Forgiveness is a release of the hurt that resulted and a signal that it's time for a new chapter.

Handling the Grief of Divorce

WHEN ARE YOU JUST GOING TO GET OVER IT AND GET ON WITH YOUR LIFE?

If you've endured a grief-causing experience, then you've heard or felt this question from your friends and maybe even your family. The question could be as much about their needs as yours. They don't know how to relate to you in grief, but they do care about your well-being. The problem is that there is no schedule for your grief. There is prolonged, acute grief. There is sometimes deferred grief. But there is no "normal" to what you are going through. What does this mean for you? For starters, it means that in some ways you may never completely "get over it." What you need are some healthy adjustments and lessons that will help you move forward in life. You're also in a process of self-rediscovery apart from your married life. This process takes time, and your loved ones need to try to understand that.

DIVORCED GRIEF RECOVERY INVOLVES REFLECTION AND HARD EMOTIONAL WORK.

Give yourself access to the honesty of your soul. This is a risky journey. Divorced people who allow this part of their journey to happen often tell me (once safely on the other side!) that the exercise was rewarding. Part of the "aloneness" of divorce is that you are stuck with yourself! Marriage, family, and household responsibilities all keep you busy. They also can distract you from the essence of who you have become. You have changed over the years of your marriage. You are now living a new reality. You have suffered hurt and are even confronting the mixture of your own blame in the dissolution of your marriage. That is a lot to process. The movement toward reflection and adjustment will come as you work in these areas and more. Again, give yourself access.

THERE IS A DIFFERENCE BETWEEN "LONELINESS" AND "ALONENESS."

None of us wants to feel lonely. We fear loneliness, and with good reason. Divorced people can sometimes feel lonely even while surrounded by friends, coworkers, or family. This is painful and hurtful, but good doses of "aloneness" are necessary for the divorce recovery process. The introspection mentioned above requires that you be by yourself sometimes. Spend the occasional quiet night at home. Allow yourself some isolation and come to know this aloneness as a friend rather than an enemy. You have work to do, and it's okay to be alone so that you can do it. Aloneness is risky, but that risk may lead you to freedom through new self-awareness and discovery!

OUR BEST UNDERSTANDINGS OF GRIEF ACKNOWLEDGE "STAGES."
Divorced grief is similar to death grief. Whether it be Elisabeth Kübler-Ross's book, *On Death and Dying*, or some other model, there is a progression to grief. In some manner, there are shock/denial, anger, reflection, and adjustment tasks involved. You don't necessarily move through these in a consecutive pattern. You may have a messy journey along this process, meandering back and forth between the stages at times. Just as you think you're "done" with being angry, there you are—angry again! None of this will happen within a week or two, either. While most people don't become clinically depressed, some may. Your feelings are what they are. Allow yourself the full experience. Get help with it if you need to.

ONE SIZE DOESN'T FIT ALL.
You should see a common theme by now: each person's grief is as unique and individual as he or she is. Your personality, how you view life, your faith values or lack of, and the particular relational experiences you've had all factor in to what you will perceive as grief. We can wish we had a resource like *The ABC's of Getting Over Grief in One Convenient Evening*. We don't. This is not a puzzle to solve or a life treasure hunt to follow. Grief is a process to live, one feeling and insight at a time. And it is *your* process.

TIME HEALS ALL WOUNDS. IF I CAN STAY BUSY ENOUGH I WILL HEAL.
This mindset is instinctive and almost always destructive. Among other things, your divorce experience is a loss. Your grieving will wait on you if you try to busy your way through it or assume that a next love will cure what ails you. You must move toward growth that is only possible as you deal with the grief. You will need to spend enough time to unplug and reflect. That's not easy in our culture of noise, speed, and distraction. Only the kind of time well spent in reflection and helpful support will heal you. God has gifted you with resources to call upon in the form of healthy friends/family, professional counseling, well-written books, and divorce groups.

EXPRESSING THE THINGS I'M FEELING CAN'T BE HEALTHY. PEOPLE WOULDN'T BELIEVE WHAT'S INSIDE ME!
Stop fearing your feelings. As long as you push them deep inside, then you are not being constructive with them. While you must be wise and discerning about the people to whom you self-disclose, you need safe people with whom you can be truthful. There is a profound power to hearing our words leave our mouths when they are coming up out of our souls! That power may prove to be healing and even freeing. Your feelings are neither good nor bad until you act on them. Your feelings are simply yours! Don't fear them. Name them, and then explore them.

PEOPLE OF FAITH ARE NOT IMMUNE TO DIVORCE OR ITS AFTERMATH.
People of faith actually divorce at the same rate as those who declare no faith background. The notion that as a person of faith you are more of a failure is not true. And the notion that your faith should completely and always comfort your grief is not fair. The truth is that you may experience somewhat of a spiritual crisis as part of your grief journey. Your God is large enough to stay at your side even in those times. Are you upset with God? If so, admit it, and pray it! You may get well-intentioned but harmful advice or theology from your friends of faith. Receive this as graciously as you can, but filter it in light of your own belief and experience. God can walk with you through rockier spiritual terrain than you might think.

Things I Hesitate to Tell Nearly-weds!

1. *We are perfectly capable of falling in love with someone we have no business marrying.*
We've all watched romantic comedies where, in the end, everything works out well. The problem is that in real life none of us has a Hollywood scriptwriter manipulating our relationship. Bad boys are called "bad boys" for a reason. "Strong-silent" types really are silent. If she's a witch now, there's a chance she'll be a witch later. But often, the differences aren't that stark. You and the other person have widely divergent values and beliefs. You want different things out of life. You come from vastly different family backgrounds. But you *love* each other. So you marry. Sometimes, all the love in the world isn't enough to bridge the expanse between two people who started out so far apart.

2. *Contrary to what we feel, our love alone will* not *see us through life.*
Marriage is work. I'm not talking about unhealthy relationships needing work. The best of all matches still involve two independent adults. There is much to attend to. Popular today is the mystical notion that if we have to work that hard at it, then it must not be right. I would turn that around and say that if you don't work at your marriage, then sooner or later it won't be right. People also try to say God will not give you more than you can carry. It seems, though, that *life* will surely give you more than you can carry. Love and commitment are the glue, but the work and negotiation by two partners are what make a marriage happen. Life intervenes. We change. Families grow. Love must be there, but there must be more than love alone!

3. *Not every divorce can be explained away by saying that two wrong people married each other.*
While we *can* choose to marry a personality type incompatible with our own, many divorces happen even when the right two people have found each other. For myriad reasons, they begin to break agreements, do damage with competitive urges, or lose interest in the relationship. Romance is often devalued, and soon two strangers are occupying the same household. Even the memory of a once-strong love fades. Marriage is work, but it is noble work. Once a couple gets tired enough of each other that they no longer want to do that work, the marriage is in trouble. Often one reawakens enough to care but finds that the partner is too far gone to save the marriage.

4. *Eventually, people who once madly loved each other can quit caring enough to try.*
We're all familiar with the story in which two flaming lovers become mortal enemies and eventually divorce. Far more common, though, is a divorce that results from a much slower process. That process involves a gradual relational distancing. We often refer to it as "drifting apart." By allowing life, work, and even children to take precedence, some partners lose their will. This is preventable! The problem is that most folks decide they don't have the time or energy to nurture what once came so easily. Maybe the toughest life-development task for married people is navigating the turn from recreation (dating) to responsibility (married life, household, family, jobs). Somewhere in all that, some couples lose touch with each other. Others lose their marriages in the "power struggle" coined by practitioners of Imago Therapy. That is, they wake up to some mature realities about each other and begin to have conflicts at those points. In any event, slow damage can be done.

5. The person you're marrying won't be the person you wake up next to twenty-five years from now—not by a long shot.
To be fair to myself, I actually *do* tell nearly-weds this, but with a slightly different approach. If we married fairly young, we really didn't know ourselves, much less the person next to us, or whom that person might become. Life takes you places you can't foresee. You win victories and you suffer losses. Each of these shapes and reshapes you. Among adult developmental tasks is coming to grips with who you are and who you are not. There is celebration and grief in these processes. We must do the same with regard to our spouses. Things that were once important about the other are less important, and things we once did not know about each other will rise dramatically in importance.

6. Your families of origin have a far more powerful hold on you than you want to admit. Much of how you function in a marriage relationship, as well as who you are attracted to, is informed by your parents—probably more than you want to realize when you are marrying. While I do spend an entire session on families (and families of origin), premarital couples I counsel will take years to discover what they need to understand about this influence. Their roles, biases, habits, assumptions, and more are shaped from home. Are you eternally locked in to these roles? Of course not, but even the conscious choices we make to "rebel" against our family's ways are shaped by our past. As a young married, your spouse asks, "Why does your family . . . ?" And you reply, "Well, I never even thought to ask why we . . . ." This is what I mean. It's not too late to interview yourself about your family of origin and its ways—what it was and what it wasn't.

7. A healthy marriage is as much miracle as it is hard work.
When we get married, we choose our mate as best we know how. Prayerfully, we do this well. When we do, we're off to a better start (obviously) than those who choose poorly. Hopefully, with good premarital counseling and healthy emotional intelligence, both partners work at the marriage. But beyond that hard work, a mature chemistry has to develop, and both people need to hold certain negotiations sacred. As you both change with time, you work at your partnership and you renegotiate. But the longer I am married—and the more couples I work with—the more mystery I find in why some marriages work healthfully and why others don't.

8. *Similarly, some factors are simply beyond your control.*
This is different from the statement on "mystery." There are practicalities here. You cannot love for both of you; you can only love for yourself. You cannot be happy for both of you; you can only be happy for yourself. You cannot have integrity for both of you. You cannot be satisfied or interested for both of you. These are functions that each of you will have to nurture individually and then together.

Lessons from *The Bachelor*: What this "Reality" Show Can Teach Us if We Pay Attention

First of all, I have to admit I've actually watched the show. With the hatchet job I'm about to do on television's *The Bachelor* (as well as online dating web sites), let me start with the housekeeping. The first thing anybody will want to know is whether I've ever actually *watched* the show. Yes, I watched two entire seasons and parts of others. I'm embarrassed to admit this. It's like road kill. You *tell* yourself not to look and then you sneak a peek as you drive by. Actually, another analogy might fit better. Watching a season of *The Bachelor* is like watching a slow train-wreck happen. But there are some good lessons for us:

IT'S NOT REAL.
Let's keep the facts straight. The producer's job is to make a marketable television show that can be sold to a network. The network's job is to buy shows that will draw good ratings so they can sell advertisement. Therefore, the "talent's" job is to play the parts that will make compelling shows that will sell. Get it? It's not real. But people are watching in droves, and people drawn to a "reality" show like *The Bachelor* get sucked in by their hopeful, romantic sides. Let me remind us that a *real*, mature, and healthy relationship won't likely be fostered in a Petri dish like a television show where the stated objective is for some poor schmo to be handed a field of contestants and then, a few weeks later, pick out the love of his life. Real relationships can't be manufactured on the clock with an audience of cameras and producers. There's nothing remotely real about this television show. I'm sorry.

FAIRYTALES CAN COME TRUE. IT CAN HAPPEN TO YOU.
Fairytales can come true . . . if you have a scriptwriter and a big budget production team writing your life's script for you. Even these contestants lose

those assets as soon as they hear "That's a wrap!" for the last time. Summer romances rarely pan out. Long-distance relationships often struggle once the two lovers are finally confronted with living together. The romantic in me likes a good happy ending as much as anyone, but we have to know the difference between something that is real and something that is not. Viewership of *The Bachelor* this year was up more than 3 million over the previous season for a show that is several years old. We *do* like a fairytale, don't we? Or maybe we like a good train wreck. It's actually sad either way.

THE "LOOKING" MODE CAUSES RELATIONSHIPS TO OVERLOOK CRITICAL ISSUES

My divorce recovery participants don't like my position with regard to online dating. Let me add television shows like *The Bachelor*—as well as barhopping—and offend some more people. Here's my beef with these contrived attempts (online dating, dating "reality" shows," barhopping) to "find love": rarely can we set out to "find" love. The fact that one is "looking" puts the person into a mode that can skew reality. If one is looking, then one is probably willing to overlook . . . overlook a bad personality mismatch, overlook a set of values that is destined to clash, overlook life goals that can't possibly mesh. All because they're looking. Do I differentiate being "open" to love from "looking" for love? You bet!

THEY LOOK LIKE ADULTS, BUT THEY'RE PLAYING A KID'S GAME.

The Bachelor is like an expensive version of the old party game "Spin the Bottle." Young teens would spin a Coke bottle and then make out with the person to whom it ended up pointing. But nobody expected to find true love that way. Yet, this supposed reality show reinforces that one can go looking for love and expect to find it. The show actually ends with the Bachelor proposing to someone. Marriage. A real-life commitment goes to the "winning" contestant. *God, save us from our shallowness.* It's no wonder divorce rates have been so high for so long. We think love and marriage can be a game. Ask my divorce recovery participants if they think it is a game.

YOU'RE NOT THE EXCEPTION YOU THINK YOU ARE!

I have to address this from time to time. When it comes to matters of the heart, most people genuinely believe they're the exception to the norm. Guess what? Most of us aren't. You may be a smart, fully grown adult, but when it comes to love, I watch middle-age (and older!) adults act like silly teenagers at times. On an even more serious note, I watch divorced people jump from one painful ending right into a new fairytale beginning. From the safety of distance, many of us can see that they're simply repeating the same relational patterns, only this time with contestants who are virtually identical to their former spouses. Everyone thinks they can beat the odds in love. Thinking I can pull off what most others obviously can't is a dangerous game to play.

How can you say this? Millions are watching!

This is the American way. Majority rules! A dumpy middle-aged minister says *The Bachelor* is teaching us lessons through self-conviction. Sure, lots of people watch *The Bachelor*. Online dating services also have millions of clients, and folks are getting married to their supposed matches. So, one man's voice is obviously wrong. After all, We assume that so many people have to be right, but we've been wrong collectively about a lot of things: presidents, economic decisions, and social policies. Christ himself recommended that we "enter through the narrow gate. For wide is the gate and broad is the road that leads to destruction, and many enter through it. But small is the gate and narrow the road that leads to life, and only a few find it" (Matthew 7:13-14). He said this sometime before the crowd voted to kill him. Just because a bunch of folks do something doesn't make it smart.

Exclusion and Embrace

Exclusion in the Divorce Experience

If you've experienced a grief-causing loss, then you've heard or felt excluded from your friends. There are some people in your life, even groups of people, who treat you differently since your divorce. There is distance now. That could be as much about their needs as yours. You see, they don't know how to relate to you in grief, and they do care about your well-being. Another cause of *exclusion* is that friends may have related to you socially as a couple, but they don't know how to relate to you now that you're single. Still another form of exclusion may come from groups or social settings to which you don't feel you belong anymore. Often, divorced people find that they've lost close in-law relationships in the separation.

Exploring the Isolation that Divorce Has Cast upon You

Give yourself access to the honesty of your soul. This is a risky journey to take. Divorced people who allow this part of their journey to happen often tell me (once safely on the other side!) that the exercise was rewarding. Part of the "aloneness" of divorce is that you are stuck with yourself. Marriage, family, and household responsibilities keep you busy, but they can also distract you from the essence of the person you have become. You have changed over the years of your marriage. You are now living a new reality. You have suffered hurt and are even confronting the mixture of your own blame in the dissolution of your marriage. That is a lot to process. The movement toward reflection and adjustment will come as you work in these areas. Again, give yourself access to the truth of your feelings.

Volf's Studies on "Otherness"

None of us wants to feel lonely. Dr. Miroslav Volf is a Yale theologian who has devoted much of his study to human reactions to "otherness." As a divorced person once said to me, "I know lots of people get divorces. But once mine happened, I felt like the only person in my world that was divorced. It's like I've got a scarlet 'D' on my forehead." Much human distancing happens in response to otherness. Volf gave attention to how we treat people whom we perceive as "different." "Exclusion and embrace" is his primary theme. It is important to offer embrace to those who have been excluded.

Healing while Helping Others to Heal

Especially in a consumer-driven culture, our response to much of life is to consume! Are you sad about your divorce? Go shopping to distract you. Are you feeling like you need a change in your social life? New clothes are a must. Do you like you're having a midlife crisis? A new car might be the elixir! The trouble is that none of this fills the void inside us. Henri Nouwen's concept of the "wounded healer" (also the title of one of his books) holds part of the answer. By being in a support group, we give as we are getting. By finding people in need and volunteering or helping, we give to something beyond ourselves and regain perspective about our hurt. We rediscover our value in relationships. We are reminded that our pain and disappointment is not *all* of who we are. No one would have wished your divorce upon you, but because of your experience, you might be uniquely postured to help someone else. You are now divorced. You can help others who hurt.

Embrace: What's all this talk about hugs?

Volf's concept of embrace is not about physical hugs or sex. For many in divorce, their sense of relational normalcy is skewed. For some time, perhaps, their marriage was less than healthy. One of the responses that comes with the search for "embrace" is that you learn about healthy relationships all over again. These do not have to be romantic relationships. What is healthy in a treasured friendship, or even in a healthy collegiality, can teach us much about what a healthy dating or marriage relationship would be like. We do this type of work in divorce recovery groups. Support groups foster embrace!

The Urge to "Get Back Out There"

For some of you, the easy answer for dealing with pain is simply to move ahead without looking back. Frankly, for a lot of my participants, finding the next person to date is too easy! You need to get to know yourself outside a significant relationship. Some people try to protect themselves from that kind of self-awareness by giving in to the urge to date. Jumping back "out there" feels intuitive, maybe even like a logical place to find "embrace." But the genuine embrace you need is larger than romance. You need healthy relationships and perspective!

Genuine Hope Rather than a False Sense of Optimism

Volf utilizes the American spirit of "optimism" as a vehicle for understanding the need for genuine narratives of hope. His call for honesty and accuracy in assessing life issues is helpful for churches. Rather than trying to idealize marriage, church, or personhood, a ministry like divorce recovery demands an atmosphere of genuine candor. Distraction from, or rationalization of, painful realities is not a healthy starting place for healing. Here is a key passage from his work: "Authentic Christian hope, on the other hand, is about the promise that the wrongs of the past can be set aright and that the future need not be a mere repetition of the past." (Miroslav Volf and Tammy Williams, "Narratives of Hope," *Christian Century* 115 [28 January 1998]: 86.)

Ambiguity as Part of the Journey from Exclusion to Embrace

Personal growth comes as a result of tremendous pain. Many divorced people who receive support find themselves processing the confusion that comes from powerful good attached to profound pain. They wonder how or why a loving God might try to work good within such terrible circumstances. Although many people attempt to hide their difficulties when inside a church, the reality is that a divorce ministry attracts hurting people. The opening session of a divorce program in particular usually includes the sharing of pain and bitter disappointment. As the sessions progress, all but a few participants report that they have learned valuable lessons. Some speak of insights gained that apply beyond the arena of their divorce experience. The nature of healing is that we discover horrible pain can sometimes bring surprising good. This ambiguity is a confusing but real part of life.

Marriage Helps

Seven Marriage Myths

1. *My partner knows I love him/her. After all, we got married. I don't have to say the words all the time.*
Actually, you do need to say the words, but not in ways that become cheap and mechanical. Predictability is a romance killer. For a lifetime ahead, your partner will want not only to hear but also to see and know that he/she is loved. In fact, by your living, you are telling your spouse of your love (or lack thereof) constantly. We all need to hear that we are loved and valued, and the message needs to match reality. Your consistency—and occasional creativity—in expressing married love is vital. This is what keeps romance alive!

2. *Time heals all wounds.*
This myth is pervasive in our culture. The saying seems well intentioned and harmless enough. However, many people really believe that time will somehow fix things. Try the saying this way instead: *Time* well spent *heals all wounds.* There is a big difference. Unaddressed issues have a way of waiting for you. Are you in pain? Have you been disappointed? Do your fears gnaw at you? Ask for help from professionals who have the skills you may need. Pray that God will help in renewal. Do the work and move on.

3. *Part of marrying me is accepting me for who I am.*
Let's be honest: you don't even know fully who you are. It is true that your spouse needs to know you as well as possible because you are a lot of who you're going to be. Trying to *fix* someone isn't a reliable plan. But in some important ways you will also change as time ebbs and flows. You'll discover things about yourself you never knew, and you'll confront painful shortcomings. You will even grieve realities of who you are. Hopefully you'll also celebrate and own the good things about yourself. You may not be able to be taken on as a fixer-upper, but neither will who you are right now remain

exactly the same. Here's why this is a myth—we all fall back on maladaptive behaviors, have shortcomings in need of correction, and need to learn new ways of doing things because we've made a partnership commitment in marriage. Part of that commitment is to learn and adjust, to problem-solve and compromise. You are responsible for your words and your actions. Part of getting better at marriage is being better as people.

4. *You win some, you lose some.*
You'll find differing opinions and a variety of terminologies to express opinions on this matter. Here's why I call this a myth: if one of you is keeping an emotional scorecard and perceives yourself to be on the losing side of the tally, you've got trouble. Most often, when one of you loses, you both lose. True solutions involve creative compromise. Another myth that fuels this one is that *compromise equals selling out.* Married love requires meaningful ways in which partnership reigns supreme over short-term outcomes. Losing feels bad. A "win" that leaves your partner feeling bad is bad for both of you. Will you agree on everything? Of course not. Most compromises involve giving from both sides. Partnership is the key.

5. *I know what I'm getting. I've met her mother already.*
That's nice, and your spouse will probably come to bear some visual resemblance to their parent of the same gender. You and your spouse will even embody mannerisms and ways similar to your parents'. No doubt, we bring forward many of the ways in which our parents played out their marriage roles. But as powerful as those influences are, we also leave behind some of our original family's shaping. Life will take a new couple to places they never imagined. You and your spouse owe it to each other to develop self-awareness about the influences of your upbringing. However, don't box each other into the roles and biases of home. Lovingly help each other discover the differences and similarities between your parents and yourselves. Address a few that need tuning up. Embrace the ones that work! Celebrate your uniqueness.

6. *I can make my marriage affair-proof. Affairs are sex outside of marriage. I would never do that just for sex!*
You're exactly right. Except that you're wrong. You might not do that just for sex. But affairs aren't *about* sex; they just *are* sex. Affairs and boredom come from un-met needs. Intimacies in a marriage that go without nurture cause the vulnerability that leads to affairs. Do you want to come as close as you

can to "affair-proofing" your marriage? Pay attention to your nurture of each other intellectually, romantically, sexually, spiritually, and emotionally. And never assume that you wouldn't "do that." Be careful. Be committed.

7. If marriage is this much work, then the relationship must not be real.
On the contrary, if you don't work at a relationship, then that's the one that might not be real. One of the great challenges of new marriage is in navigating a turn of the corner between recreation and responsibility. Married love should be free and easy in some ways, but a mature relationship between two whole people requires some work. Do you need skilled, third-party help from a counselor or therapist? Reach out for that help. Grow your love and move forward together.

Finding "Me" without Losing "Us"

How do I find "me" without losing "us"?
Some couples appear to change seamlessly across the decades of their marriages. Their subtle shifts occur with no signs of stress. But no one knows what goes on behind their closed doors! We know that some couples struggle. One young woman reached out for help by asking for a counselor. Eventually, she voiced her anxiety about "moving from being a student to being a wife with responsibilities and a new identity to establish." Another had an affair with a seventeen-year-old, and then another later with someone their own age. In that case, the affairs were the results of a delayed adolescence. A developmental issue in marriage is constructively finding "me" without losing "us" over the years. That's how Robert Herron, a counselor in North Carolina, expresses this.

Self-awareness is the answer, and it's not easy.
A starting place is in your level of commitment to "us." Viewing your marriage as a partnership can be a powerful driver of how you self-maintain. In a healthy partnership, one somehow holds on to the value that no issue or challenge will be allowed to break down the partnership. When that value is in place, how you address problems is different. One spouse came to her partner. She had been suffering silently with generalized anxiety that was not rooted in marital trouble, but she valued her partnership enough to understand that her pain was beginning to affect the home. She gathered up the courage it took to express her problems, and then asked her partner to walk

with her as she got help. Not only did he support her in counseling, but oddly their relationship emerged stronger for having weathered the crisis together. However, they will journey with those issues to some degree for the rest of their lives.

YOU WON'T BE THE SAME PERSON AT 45 AS YOU WERE AT 25.
The basics of who you have become as an adult will remain, but life will take you different places. You achieve and you fail. You have children or you don't. The meandering path of life takes you through gain and loss. Along the way, new insights come, and self-awareness increases. You grieve some of what is and some of what is not. You celebrate what you've become and revel in the serendipity of what you never expected. None of this leaves you unaffected. Add in some of the behaviors, thoughts, or biases you'll develop along the way, and you are altered as you live. A good marriage becomes something to be celebrated as two humans move along together. A healthy marriage will need open communication, lovingly practiced each day in order to stay a healthy marriage.

EVEN YOU DON'T KNOW WHAT YOU DON'T KNOW.
An academic mentor warned me about my marriage and divorce work years ago. His caution was about burnout. Instinctively, I knew he could be right. But I now know that one season of that burnout has presented itself in an odd way: I am managing a growing pessimism about my premarital couples actually being ready to get married. Here's the problem—many of us get married at an age when we don't even know ourselves. Much less can our spouses know us deeply at that point. I don't want to suggest that young couples shouldn't marry, but I do want to caution them to live and love together with sensitivity and openness and to choose wisely! Pay attention to relational warning signs. Your spouse deserves for you to have few "secrets" in your lifetime. Work together, explore together, and ask questions together! Support each other as you discover and as you shape each other. If you're considering marriage to someone who won't do these things—think about it some more.

HEED THESE WARNING SIGNS CAREFULLY!
Couples marry and almost immediately begin a transition from a predominantly recreational life to one more rooted in responsibility. I know you love each other; now take a good look at your partner. Look deep within them at what you know. That's all you can work with. Is there something about them

that would be a deal-breaker if you didn't want to get married so badly? Here are a few specific questions: Do I suspect my spouse has kept a serious "secret" from me—monetarily, relationally, morally, or other? Is there what seems like a clinical personality disorder that I've so far chosen to overlook? Does one or the other of us have frequent disinterest in what the other is saying/doing? Am I having a prolonged attraction to a friend, neighbor, or coworker? Is there sudden, unexplained anger toward my partner? Do I feel depressed? Am I disinterested in my partner touching me? Can I be married to this person, or stay married to this person, without some help with one or more of these issues? Is my partner struggling with one or more of these feelings toward me?

CONSIDER THE HALLMARKS OF A HEALTHY RELATIONSHIP.

No doubt you want to hear some good news. If you've addressed the scary stuff listed above, consider these questions that might indicate a healthy place for *you* to be *you*: Does your partner help you feel free to be you? Does your relationship empower you rather than hold you back? Do you and your partner communicate regularly, deeply, and constructively? Does your relationship leave you both room to express your talents and personal callings in life? As challenges arrive, do you feel safe in expressing them to your partner? Can you ask your partner for help? Do you and your partner have healthy, balanced relational expectations that you have negotiated and shared? Does your partner, by being who they are, challenge you in some way to be a better person?

ISN'T THIS A LOT TO WORRY ABOUT?

The last thing I want to do is to cause couples to over-think and over-worry about their relationships! On some level, I am not overly concerned about that. Most couples could stand to do a more introspection before taking their vows. A way to misuse these Marriage Helps resources is to develop a passel of checklists or to begin obsessing over an issue that isn't yours. I don't want to suggest you toward a problem that isn't there, but I do want to move you toward healthy awareness that there is work to be done if you are to be a satisfied "you" within a thriving "us." Couples who need to do some work, but don't, get into trouble. Live and love as open partners. Don't over-think your love! But live in the awareness that help is out there. Get that help if you need it, and nurture your love.

Competitors or Lovers?

Curb the destructive power of competitiveness in marriage.

BUT WE DIDN'T START OUT THAT WAY . . .

Of course you didn't. There's no cookie-cutter set of motivations or patterns that leads down the road to a hurtful level of competition between husbands and wives. Personalities differ, and you bring differing backgrounds from your families of origin. You have diverse ways of dealing with the things that happen in life. But consider these questions:

- To what standard of decency and love will you hold each other?
- How much pain can your love withstand and still remain healthy?
- How can you process the quandaries or frustrations of life in ways that respect each other?
- From the beginning, have you negotiated the right to hold each other accountable for behavior that is out of bounds?

No one starts out intending to hurt a spouse. Years of accumulated pain, and a sense of losing, can take a toll on a relationship.

WHAT EXACTLY IS MARITAL "COMPETITION"?

For our purposes, "competition" has a couple of features that should make sense to you. First, we'll assume that competition arises mostly under pressure or anger. Competition might not be your primary way of relating, but when pushed, you may revert to a different relational style. Related, the competitive relationship finds pressure or anger reactions turning regularly toward the need to "win." The win becomes more important than the original issue. In fact, sometimes you may even lose sight of what started it all. For some reason, the need to get your "say" or have your way drives you.

COMPETITORS GO FOR THE WIN AT ALL COSTS.

That's the problem—the costs are tremendous. Competition between husband and wife removes vast relational capital from your storehouse. Competition costs you trust. The need to be "right" causes your spouse to tire of your presence at times. This atmosphere costs your partner some pieces of his or her self-esteem. On some level, you may not even respect yourself. If you have children, they're watching and learning! Is winning worth the inevitable losses?

Competitors don't care who the audience is.

"Praise in public, discipline in private" is working-world wisdom. More supervisors should know this rule and go by it! So should more spouses. Competitiveness that has taken root in a marriage often plays out in front of the kids, the friends, and the family. Eventually, no one cares who is watching or listening, at least until the issue has passed. Then the horror of the drama sets in. Awkward conversations ensue, bringing anger, frustration, and loss of self-esteem. Is any of this building a better marriage for anybody? Not likely. Are public displays wearing on your relationship? You bet! And damaging each other in front of others exacts more relational tolls—including what happens with your friends or family who may love you but dread wondering when the next drama will suck them in again!

You deserve better.

You both do! You deserve better than to be in constant competition with your spouse. One of the steps toward awakening is to draw from your self-esteem and realize that you deserve better than to live in a disappointing, embarrassing, and damaging pattern. You and your spouse signed on for a lifetime of marriage. You promised to be the presence of Christ to each other. Instead, competition sucks the love out of the relationship. Competition postures spouses as rivals who threaten and cannot be trusted at a fulfilling level. Whether your competition is nearly constant or occasionally hurtful, you can work toward new and rewarding ways of loving each other. One of the crucial tasks, though, is owning the notion that *you* deserve better, and especially knowing that your partner deserves the best possible you.

Do we have to agree on everything?

Of course not; expecting to agree on everything simply is not realistic. Married partnership is not about always being on the same page. In fact, one test of a healthy partnership is how you handle the times in life when you're absolutely at *odds* with each other. No couple can see 100 percent of life in the same way. It's just that your relationship is the one arena where a lifetime of enrichment counts on your respectful disagreement. Partnership demands that you find ways to differ and to problem-solve so that you move on meaningfully. You have a busy and complicated life. Your energy and resources need to be aimed at managing that demanding life, not jettisoned off in wasted and hurtful competition with each other.

KNOW WHEN TO ASK FOR HELP.
The toxic competitive relationship may need professional help. Earlier, you read that competition often arises as a relational style to which you revert either under pressure or in anger. You may need help unpacking why your spouse has consistently become a source of anger. This starting place may need the skilled exploration that a trusted counselor or therapist can provide. You must begin by identifying your pattern of reverting to anger or competition. Because your way of relating has become comfortable, this level of self-awareness may be more difficult than you could imagine. There is an irony at work—the very target of your anger or competitiveness may be the one in the best position to hold you accountable for the pattern. In a relationship where habitual and toxic competition has taken root, they may not have the permission to raise the issue. This is a problem. Can the two of you permit yourselves to "mirror" lovingly for the other?

COMMIT TO BREAKING THE CYCLE.
A wife and mother sobbed in my office. She said, "I don't want to live like this. I don't want our kids to see us like this!" That was the breakthrough moment. She had awakened by way of seeing the destruction she and her husband had left in their wake. In their unique ways, they had fallen into a pattern of "going at each other" as an early and often way of dealing with their differences. They embarrassed themselves, pushed loved ones away from them, and risked embedding this pattern of relating in their young children. But when those images connected with her, she got it! Her spouse had seen the pattern a little earlier, but it takes two to tame the competition beast. They set to work on it, armed with new boundaries and covenants they both could own. They continue to seek new ways of interacting. Frankly, a primary aim is to move back in the direction of the respectful love they shared as a dating couple.

Critical Issues That Get in the Way of Healthy Marriages

COMPETITIVENESS DOES MORE DAMAGE THAN YOU REALIZE.
Two adults move into life as independent persons. They find each other. Love blossoms. A fairy-tale wedding takes place, with vows to partner and to support one another. They intend well. Then, having taken on a "roommate for life," they begin to keep score. *We got the color car you wanted. Well, I have to see your parents more than I get to see mine. Hey, we always take the kind of*

vacation you like. By then, both are trying to "fix" the other, to smooth off the rough edges they knew were there but that weren't a big enough deal not to get married. Now they're into the silent game of *I'm tired of you bossing me.* Or a match of *I'm going to get my way this time!* Committed couples see instead the damage competitiveness can do. They address the insecurities and annoyances. They come to the agreement that competition or rivalry hurts a marriage. Being the presence of Christ means wanting to forge a marital culture where neither of you feels like a rival. Do this work early and often. Stave off the damage of competitiveness. Get help if you need it!

CONSUMERISM SHAPES MORE THAN HOW YOU SPEND YOUR MONEY.
America transformed toward a "consumer" culture as the economy kicked into gear after World War II. A few generations later this silent, shaping force in our lives has us all thinking like consumers. Some try to do church as consumers of a spiritual body's goods and services. Some try to do careers as consumers of what the companies "owe" the workers. All too many approach marriage unwittingly shaped as consumers. This bent toward your partner needing to fit into *your* patterns, preferences, biases, schedule, or wants is obviously imbalanced. When you exchanged vows, you both signed a figurative "waiver" on the universe getting to revolve around either of you! Yet that's how some people attempt to live as married partners. Self-awareness is the starting place. Open dialogue with your partner may be a need. Managing yourself, and both partners holding each other mutually accountable, may be a key. Married partners give—and take. Are you doing a healthy amount of both?

A LACK OF CREATIVITY IS HARMFUL.
You'll read elsewhere in these Marriage Helps that "creativity" is a key to nurturing healthy romance. So it is. But the need for creativity applies far more broadly than the area of romance. Couples sometimes forget to muster their creativity when resolving conflict or trying to make a tough decision. Taking the time to brainstorm may be your best action when working on a household management challenge that has you befuddled. But couples get so busy! The mentality is that they need to work harder or faster. Taking the time and effort to listen and work together "creatively" may be more important than getting something done! Creativity takes time. Creativity takes intentional planning at times. Isn't that ironic? The pay-off comes when you do something different or better.

MARRIED COUPLES NEED SKILLS SETS FOR RESOLVING CONFLICT, BREAKING PATTERNS, AND MAKING DECISIONS.
The business world got this one right: the definition of insanity really *can* be doing the same thing over and over, yet expecting different results. Here's another business saying: if the only thing you carry in your toolbox is a hammer, then every problem begins to look like a nail. Every couple I work with in marriage tune-up or in premarital counseling has to do a homework session in conflict resolution. There are specific communication, management, and partnering skills needed to work together in the challenges of life. It's not enough just to talk. Your talking has to involve intentional creativity, negotiation, brainstorming, and a shared set of clear values in order to unlock the heaviest problems. Many couples arrive at marriage ill equipped to do these. (Another Marriage Helps page speaks to this in more detail.)

PAY ATTENTION TO ROMANCE.
Couples let go of romance for many reasons: we had kids, our careers are demanding, our relationship has matured beyond all that. Some simply say, "There's just no time." Guess what? Everybody still wants to feel special in the eyes of their spouse. Neglect of romance leads to the opposite. Most couples don't set out to lose their "spark." They simply let it happen over time. Don't! Take back your right to romance as a couple. Figure out what you need from each other. Hold your partner up as important enough to invest the effort. If you both try, you both win!

KNOW YOUR PERSONALITY TYPE AS A COUPLE.
I've become convinced that it helps for married people to know about their "personality type" as a couple. We know that individuals have unique personalities, but do you really know who you are as a couple? As a unit, you have capabilities and limitations. You have biases and habits. You have priorities and missions that are unique to you as a twosome. This kind of self-awareness might help you to hone your vision, achieve what you want to achieve, and not set yourselves up for disappointment.

MAINTAIN THE SENSE OF "WANT-TO."
This one comes almost last because this critical issue is where I find couples in deep trouble. When you damage your relationship or find you have pushed each other away, you can lose the "want-to" that is needed to do the healthy work of marriage. In our culture, we often refer to this as "we grew

apart." It's the sense that you didn't set out to watch your marriage dissolve, but now you don't have the emotional energy it would take to try to heal it. It takes two of you to try! Couples have to work at their marriages ahead of arriving in this state. In a healthy relationship, you view your spouse as someone worth the effort. You hold your marriage in that level of priority. In an unhealthy relationship, you find it hard to muster the will to start something new or to revive an old habit that once worked well for the two of you. This sense of "want-to" is a large part of what's at stake in your enrichment work.

MAINTAIN TRUST.
Similar to "want-to," a loss of trust can eventually happen in a damaged relationship. The work of a healthy marriage assumes that both partners trust each other. When you betray your partner's trust by violating key intimacies, you do lasting damage. When you disrespect each other and try to control each other, you damage trust. I tell my couples that when they fight, it's never just about what they're fighting over. I would argue that even more important, they are banking or burning valuable personal capital with each other. Yes, you can disagree agreeably! When you do, you teach each other about what you can depend on.

Stuck Trying to Resolve a Specific Conflict?
Wanting to Break a Pattern of Behavior That's Not Working?
Got a Tough Decision You Can't Figure Out How to Make?

1. *The business world got this one right—the definition of insanity really is doing the same thing over and over, but expecting new and different results.*
Yet to be human is to live in patterns. This is never truer than in relationships. Sometimes our patterns work fine. Other times, not so much. We learned some of our life patterns as young children. Mostly, we learned them in response to times when we didn't get what we wanted or when we didn't feel loved. Some of them work better for us than others. Counselors refer to the ones that don't work well as maladaptive behaviors or schema. The moments of self-awareness where we know we need to try something new are when growth happens in marriages. Here's another saying: If it gets you what you want, do more of it. If it doesn't, then maybe it's time to renegotiate and be more creative.

2. Sometimes, to get to the solution you have to first negotiate the values that will become criteria.
Sorry if this doesn't sound like much fun. There are situations in life where racing toward a decision or a solution won't get you where you need to be. Knowing when to listen to each other about what is important may be the key to unlocking potential solutions. It's better to be clear about what's important to each other before rushing toward an outcome. You'd rather have the right solution than the fast one most of the time. There's time later to arrive at the one you wanted, and you'll see it more clearly if you've invested the effort in defining some criteria.

3. Conflict resolution assumes trust.
That is, *both* parties must trust each other equally. Another assumption is that you as an individual are worthy of being trusted. (By the way, your ability to trust your partner will be affected by your own level of self-trust!) While there are differences, you both value an outcome that is best for the big picture of your relationship. If that trust level isn't present, then there is some work to do. Talk. Listen. Repair if need be. This is one of those aspects where the only healthy relational outcomes happen when there are two willing parties. One of you can't do this alone.

4. Will the same business skills that make you a champion in your career(s) see you successfully through married life?
Some of what makes you formidable in the workplace, or skilled at your job, will serve you well. Among many other realities, marriage is signing on to run a company called "us." There are business aspects where your specific savvy will be exactly what carries the day. But especially when dealing with your partner, some of your strengths can also become weaknesses when overplayed. Used to excess, what works at work might not work at home! Your spouse isn't a board of directors to be manipulated, a jury to be convinced, or a poor vendor to be beaten down. Remember the saying—if all you carry in your toolbox is a hammer, then every problem starts to look like a nail. Don't play your spouse for a cheap "win." Don't manage your loved one in order to get your way. Your partner can learn to sense when he or she is being handled by you. Treat each other fairly and with integrity.

5. The only way out is the way through.
Conflict or tough decisions can test your commitment. In sloppy relationships, there is often one spouse who gets frustrated and pushes the nuclear

button. "Well, then I ought to leave you!" Or "Fine, maybe we should get a divorce!" When this is something you'll toss into the fray, then it's an option for you. This is a dangerous game to play. Eventually one of you comes to see that outcome as a better potential solution than the hard work needed to pull things together. But when two people are equally committed, there is a chance at the creativity and trust needed to dislodge tough impasses.

6. *Brainstorming is to be understood—and then put to work in these marriage situations.*
True brainstorming is a skill. If there is one skill that couples are often a little short on, it's brainstorming. We're all busy and pressed for time. Often, we jump into a competition to get our particular idea heard. We want our partner to "listen" to us, which for most of us means seeing a situation our way. Brainstorming is a skill that, when utilized by couples, facilitates open discussion, creative thought, and active listening. Here's the rule: when brainstorming, all ideas are good ideas! If a couple keeps this sacred between them, then brainstorming works. Take a blank sheet of paper and jot down your ideas; debriefing them or arguing over their validity is against the rules. You've got time later to move on and begin evaluating potential solutions. Still later, you can eliminate a few ideas (according to the criteria you share). Finally, you can choose the one or two solutions to which you'll both commit equally.

7. *A win-lose scenario isn't true to life.*
I mean that literally. In a marriage, it will be rare that when one of you loses you don't both lose. There's not much justice in watching your spouse lose. Sometimes, you might both be better off losing in some ways than trying to live with an outcome where one clearly wins at the bitter expense of the other's loss. Remember—business rules don't always apply. Emotionally, when your spouse loses you've also lost.

8. *Compromise does not equal sell-out.*
The Washington, DC, politicians got this one right. Politics is the art of compromise. You don't think your home is political? Put this article down and walk away. Don't come back until you rid yourself of this myth. Here's the problem: some of us has been enculturated to think compromise causes us to give up parts of who we are that we can't afford to lose. This brings me to my final thought.

9. *There is no one issue that is worth doing damage to your relationship.*
Remember this above all else. People lose sight of this principle too easily. In the heat of the moment, or in the drag of old business, perspective is easy to lose. Your fight over a seemingly large issue can't be handled in sloppy or unfair ways that damage your relationship. That's why having boundaries in place is vital. Knowing the language of your conflict, as well as the pace of your resolution, are musts.

Does Your Spouse Think You're Emotionally Available?

Connection doesn't just happen. Here are some things you can do that help.

ARE YOU EVER THERE BUT NOT REALLY THERE?

You can tell when you are "there" with someone and when you've tuned them out. Likewise, we have a sense about when someone has tuned us out, too. Why do some husbands and wives operate on that wavelength as a normal course of life? Not exactly 100 percent of what we say to each other is a life-and-death issue. Still, we find that connections don't always happen at times when something does matter. Even worse than momentary misfires is the loneliness that can result when a relationship becomes disconnected. Teach each other good, healthy, active listening skills. Brainstorm the language that clues each other in as to the "importance level" of a conversation. Be willing to tell your spouse that you're not feeling connected at a given moment rather than settling for a one-sided conversation. Discuss not only the importance of connection, but the relational implications of availability. Don't live with loneliness. Ask for the gift of presence. Give it, too.

GUYS DON'T WRITE "THINKING OF YOU" NOTES.

But maybe they should. I'm not a nature guy, nor am I a nurture guy. I happen to think that both are involved. I also believe that in providence and creativity, God made us all uniquely. There is some basic wiring that is different in all of us. Some of us are more inclined to patience, while others are more passionate or have shorter fuses. Still others are loving and even nurturing. Then there's the socialization part. This influence of who raised us, and how they did it, seems equally valid in understanding personalities. When you sign on to love in a committed relationship, you sign on in part to let your partner know they are important to you. This involves words at times. Loving demands connection and active listening. We need feedback and cooperation from our spouses. We have to function in active ways with each other. For some of us, that may mean smoothing off some of the edges of who we are or tweaking our "nature/nurture" in other ways. Our spouses may need some things from us that we have to learn to give. What is your spouse asking of you?

WISH LISTS TEACH GOOD SKILLS.
One of the exercises in working couples through the counseling sessions I do is to have them go home and fill out a "wish list." My theory has long held that by the time a couple comes in front of me for premarital counseling, they already have a "fixer-upper" list on each other. This is even truer with couples who have been married a while. I get them to write at least three things they wish their partners would do more often. During the next session, we spend the hour debriefing their requests of each other. The point is to practice assertive language instead of letting things build to the point of aggressive talk that is hurtful, or passive aggressive efforts that are insulting. A degree of healthy partnership is simply in serving as a gauge for each other. Talk it over. Will you give each other a sense of permission to sound the alarm when you see a need for adjustment?

TALK WITH EACH OTHER . . . YOU CAN DO IT.
When Elizabeth and I realized we were serious in our relationship, the joke was that in five years we wouldn't need any words! While we were acknowledging a connection, the sad news is that there are couples that arrive at about five years of marriage and are already trying to get by on few if any words. In reading all of these Marriage Helps pages, you could become exhausted if you viewed each suggestion as an isolated or individual act. But when placed in the context of a loving, committed relationship, much of what you find here should happen as two loving partners interact. Communication is the most essential element of a healthy relationship. Like refreshing water poured on a thirsting soul, God gave us the ability to communicate so that relationships can be sustained. How do we start? By starting. Go ahead. Talk. You can do it.

YOU REALLY DO HAVE THE TIME.
It is a foregone conclusion that people are busy these days. Be careful about giving in too easily to time distractions. Are you too busy to be with the one you've pledged to love? Too busy to have conversations, to work creatively in solving difficulties? Too busy to nurture romance so that you won't empty

the memory account of your dating years in stunningly short order? Some of us waste inordinate amounts of time without realizing it. Then we say we "didn't have time" to do some things we should have done. I've found another truism—we make time for the things that are really important to us. Isn't your marriage commitment one of the most important parts of your life? Investing time with your spouse is not optional. Enjoy quality and quantity of time as you can.

KNOW WHEN TO ASK FOR HELP.
At some point, you and your spouse may move past the point where self-maintenance will help you with emotional availability. You may need to ask for help. Sometimes the people who need good counseling or therapy are the last to allow it. Many marriages fall into disrepair but could be redeemed. Please be willing to fight for your married love by working at it. Find skilled third-party help who can lead you to bridge the gaps in your emotional connection. Wishing it so will not make it so. If your ministers are like me, they know skilled professionals with whom they would entrust you. Let them get you the help you need while you still care enough to do the work.

Money Matters

Sound financial partnership is key to managing the company called "us."

1. *Manage your money so that it doesn't manage you!*
This first principle sounds like a cheesy line you would expect to see pop up on a PowerPoint slide in a corporate training seminar. But this one is simple and true. When you manage your money effectively, you have more options for how to respond to life's surprises. You also have more flexibility to live your dreams and your sense of calling in life. Conversely, there is nothing sadder than someone stuck in a job they hate simply because they can't afford to do anything else. For couples, money management takes constant and healthy communication and the utmost in integrity. Shared visions, commitment to sound money policies, and a willingness to work together creatively are also essential. Are you willing?

2. *Budgets are the starting place (but only the starting place).*
Couples need to budget in order to know how to make financial decisions. Most couples who come to me for marriage work confess that budgets confuse them. I suggest that budgets only lead us to spending agreements in

married life. It isn't the budget that will control your spending. A budget is only a blueprint for what you want to do. An agreement that you will both live up to is what will govern how you actually spend your money. Move beyond budgets to action plans and promises. Make them realistic. Make them sacred. Make them now.

3. *Spending policies have to be negotiated early and then followed with integrity.* Each couple may have unique needs, but there are general patterns. (1) What is important for us to save for? (2) Will those savings be so important that we "pay ourselves first" for them? (3) How much unaccountable money (allowance) can we each get? (4) What is the most money I can spend without having to talk first with my spouse? (5) Can either of us access a savings account for a purpose other than it is designated for without first consulting the other? There are more: Who carries the checkbook? Or do we even use a checkbook? Who balances the records? How often do we sit down together to look at our total financial picture?

4. *Save for retirement—now and later.*
Newlyweds seem to find any mention of "retirement" to be irrelevant. They're just starting out, and there are wedding expenses and maybe even school loans to pay for. There's a house to save for, and retirement seems far off. Let me break the news to you gently: unless you're gambling that you'll be the next Bill and Melinda Gates, retirement saving starts now. Sit down with your human resources representative and let them show you the charts for the person who starts saving late in life versus the person who starts early. Saving for college for your little one? Some money experts even recommend that retirement savings must take a higher priority than college. Take it seriously, and start saving soon!

5. *The dramatic power of money invites outsiders into the privacy of your home.* Divorcing people in our country perceive money to be the number one cause of marital strife. While the interpretations of such responses should be addressed more fully, let's follow their perception. Money troubles have a unique power in marriage. For one thing, you as an individual are subject not only to your own challenges with money but also to your spouse's spending habits. When you owe someone money, it feels as if your creditors have moved in with you. Money secrets violate integrity issues between spouses, too. A spouse who finds she has been misled may start to wonder if there are other areas besides money she should question as well. Managing money

reduces the power that others have in your personal life. Managing money helps a couple to feel independent and fulfilled.

6. Congratulations! You just married each other's assets—and the liabilities too.
One sweet bride voiced a concern that her fiancé was about to "marry" her old student loans. She felt guilty about him having to share in her debt. Another was stressed because she still had car payments and her fiancé was driving a car that was already paid for. Such fairness concerns are encouraging but perhaps misplaced. When we marry our spouses, we marry more than their families. We marry their financial pictures, too. No matter how a couple may manage their books, they are still dealing with a finite pool of resources. They need to work together to manage the demands on those resources so that their collective vision can come true. The time for surprises is before the wedding. After the wedding, it's time to get down to the ongoing negotiations for how to manage a company called "us"!

7. Newer couples may be the wealthiest they'll ever be.
This is a philosophical point. When I get a young couple in premarital counseling, I've often got a blank financial slate. Most of my couples have not yet bought/rented the place where they plan to live. They're driving cars that are still not overly expensive. Now is the time for them to fold together two financial realities and emerge with a new unified one. Together, they have a chance to negotiate and dream. They still have the chance to avoid living in too much house, driving too much car, and maybe even having too much wedding! When they can set up their lives realistically, they live on less than they make and move toward what's important to them. That's financial wealth by most of the world's standards.

8. Americans recently spent more than they made.
In a year recently completed, Americans averaged spending $.01 more than they earned per dollar. This is the first time this has happened since the Great Depression. You don't have to be a mathematical or financial genius to know that this cannot work. You can do better, but it will take your best communication and creativity to live above consumer greed. Talk with your partner and figure out how to tame the consumption beast.

Relating to Your Families of Origin

OUR FAMILIES ARE POWERFUL SHAPERS OF WHO WE ARE.
We think that when we grow up, we are our "own" people. But there we are in the office doing things like we did them at home when our older sibling was ordering us around. Or we say something one of our parents would've said and then wonder, "Where did that come from"? Beginning at surprisingly early ages, we are formed powerfully by the roles we play in our families of origin. Some even theorize that the imprint of how our parents act out their marital/parental roles affects how we enact those roles in our own adulthoods. Are we hopelessly affixed like puppets to these roles and images? Of course not. But realizing the driving influences in our lives is a key to self-awareness. Self-awareness is the beginning of being intentional about how we relate to our partners. Celebrate the healthy qualities you brought with you! As for the other stuff, at least now you can work on it too.

EVEN THE STUFF WE REBEL AGAINST (AND LEAVE BEHIND) COMES FROM THEM.
Being late for baseball practice or church for the umpteenth time pushed me to embarrassment. It frustrated me. From middle-school age, I swore that "some day" I wouldn't be late everywhere I went. Now, a good schedule is like a security blanket to me. I love being early, tolerate being on time, and detest being late (on the rare occasions when I allow it to happen). As kids, we start keeping a list of things we're going to do differently from the way our parents did them. Some of those things fall off the list as we get older and our parents suddenly get smarter. There are other patterns and biases that we do intentionally leave behind as we chart our own relational courses. Here's the important thing to remember: even those behaviors we take on because of what we leave behind are actually shaped by our families of origin. As an independent adult, you are still being shaped by your parents and siblings.

WHERE ARE YOU GOING TO CELEBRATE CHRISTMAS THIS YEAR?
At some point, most premarital couples I work with get a question from me like, "So, where are you going to be this Christmas day"? The question is usually met with much glancing back and forth and stammering. Candidly, I don't care where they're going to be this Christmas, as long as it involves them being in the sanctuary for our Christmas Eve service. The point is that questions like this one are going to be real-life issues for them. They'll have

to negotiate as they relate to their families of origin. Birthdays, anniversaries, celebrations, bereavement, and holidays call upon us to work out practical and fulfilling solutions with our partners. The quest is to relate to our families in a healthy sense of balance that might never be perfect. How will you make decisions like that? Carefully and sensitively with your partner is a start. Listen to each other, and discover what is truly important to both of you.

BE THE AMBASSADOR WITH YOUR OWN FAMILY.

When talking about our relationships with family, I advise my couples to be the liaison with their own families of origin. At the engagement celebration, Dad wrapped his arms around you and said to forget the "in-law" designation. Mom says your husband is now the son she's always wanted! They meant this, except when you break bad news to your partner's family. Or maybe when he tells your folks "no" to the invitation they assumed you couldn't wait to receive. Handle the difficult situations with your own family, and let your spouse do the same with his or hers.

ASK EACH OTHER QUESTIONS ABOUT YOUR FAMILIES.

This is especially important because your spouse will have questions about your family you haven't even thought to ask yet. You must give each other permission to ask! Let your taboos be few and far between with your spouse. They deserve to know. Likewise, they have to be sensitive in how they ask you those questions. These sorts of exchanges are treasure troves of information that explain you and help your spouse understand your family system. Asking questions, telling stories, even explaining the unexplainable will help your spouse know how to be a part of your family. You'll also be caused to think through issues you haven't yet explored. Be gentle, but be open to each other.

CAN YOUR SPOUSE GET "IN" TO YOUR FAMILY?

As I write this, I've just met with a young couple. She comes from a small, quiet family. She's an only child, and she has just one aunt/uncle with no children. Everybody is good to each other, but family gatherings are less frequent and low-key when they happen. The groom comes from a large family with an even larger extended family. Their gatherings are loud, direct, and robust. He finds it quiet and awkward at her family get-togethers. She used the word "overwhelming" three times when describing his family. They have work to do in helping each other get "in" to each other's families. Help your spouse understand the dynamics and the politics of your family. Ask questions about theirs. Visit with each other until your partner gets used to being around your family. Help each other find a place in the other family, while also retaining your unique personhood in the mix.

Worksheets

Can We Start a Divorce Recovery Ministry at Our Church?

Not to make this work sound too simplistic, but I believe three conditions are helpful for starting a support group or Bible study class. Let's say you have two of the three, but come up short on the other. If so, wait. Get that last condition met, or you could be in for a tough trek. You need these three conditions to start a group:

• *Opportunity.* There must be people in your church, or people with whom you have relationships in the community, who are a part of the constituency to whom you wish to minister. In this case, that would be actual divorced people who are willing to participate in a divorce recovery support group. Some of the best groups I've had lately may only have as many as four participants. But even with three people, it is difficult to sustain a group over two months' time.

• *Resources.* You need the budget, facilities, and know-how to start such a ministry. Resources also include the collection of print or electronic material that you will need to guide the sessions. Don't overlook the obvious. Publicity will cost at least a minimal amount of money. Your church or group will have to be committed enough to spend start-up money. Fees should be structured for cost recovery, but you may have to offer a "scholarship" for the occasional participant for whom money is an obstacle.

• *Leadership.* A new support group requires appropriate, skilled, trained, and talented leaders who will be effective. Sometimes, however, the more willing people may not be the right ones! You will get volunteers who are less than ideal, so be careful about publicizing your need for leaders. Instead, you will likely have to recruit aggressively to get the right people on board. Who are the "right" people? Chief among their attributes is a willingness to set their own needs aside and remain in the role of a facilitator. Also, they'll need to be adept in leading the discussion so that it doesn't go places that are beyond the intent of a support group. They'll also need to be capable of balancing group participation—not allowing any one person to do all the talking, and encouraging those who rarely speak to share.

All three of these vital conditions must be accounted for, or you should rethink your eagerness to begin. Despite the best intentions, you may need to postpone the ministry vision until more work can be done! This worksheet may help you make a decision about your proposed group.

1. Do we have a ready *opportunity*, or do we simply have a ministry vision? List the reasons for your answer.

_____

_____

If you only have a vision at this point, what will it take to have a real opportunity?

_____

_____

What is a realistic timetable to create an opportunity? Why?

_____

_____

2. What *resources* make us ready to start a support group now?

_____

_____

What resources do we still lack? Why?

_____

_____

What will it take for us to get these resources?

_____

_____

Who will be responsible for overseeing the gathering of resources?

_____

3. What attributes are we looking for in our *leadership* for this ministry?

_____

_____

Who meets these qualifications?

_____

_____

If we are short on leadership for now, what will we have to do in order to find the right people?

_____

_____

Ad Copy (for church newsletter, web site, newspaper, etc.)

Divorced or Separated?
Looking for perspective?

A place for healing

8 Wednesdays beginning September 26 at 6:15 pm
Fee: $50 per person

Call Lisa Lynch to pre-register or with questions at 404-266-8111
Pre-registration deadline: September 23
http://www.spdl.org/divorce.html

Second-Ponce de Leon Baptist Church
2715 Peachtree Road
Atlanta, GA 30305

Welcome Flyer (for participants' Resource Book we provide)

Welcome to Divorce Recovery at Second-Ponce de Leon Baptist Church!

While this is a painful time in your life, we are honored that you are spending this portion of your healing effort with us. We hope that you will feel comfortable here among us.

Here are some tidbits that you might be wondering about:

• Our program begins at 6:30 pm and ends by 8:00. We'll be prompt, especially in consideration of our childcare and building personnel. The fee is $50, payable to: Second-Ponce de Leon Baptist Church (memo line- *Divorce Recovery*). We'll run eight (8) weeks, meeting each Wednesday night. The fee includes your book, *Growing through Divorce*, by Jim Smoke.
• Attendance is vital to our experience. You are adults. Attendance cannot be mandated. Part of your journey to recovery is built on your willingness to follow through on commitments you make with others. Your fellow participants will rely on you to be present in order for the group to be all that it can be. Everyone will have something that causes him or her to miss a session. However, please make it a priority to attend as many sessions as possible. Others are counting on you.

- In case of inclement weather, please call our church office at 404-266-8111. In the event of closure and program cancellation, we will have a special recorded greeting. It will not reference the divorce recovery program specifically, but it will advise you that events are cancelled or altered. Call the number during the afternoon in order to get the most up-to-date information.
- Our Wednesday evening meal is served from 5 pm until 6:15. Reservations are not necessary. The fellowship hall is located just upstairs as you enter the main building. Please feel free to take advantage of the meal if it will help you make your schedule work better. We hope you'll enjoy the fellowship!
- We offer this opportunity for you as a part of your healing. It is available for our church members, but most participants will be from the broader community. As such, we will not push the general program of our church unduly. However, you are welcome at all church activities. We would love to talk further about Second-Ponce de Leon Baptist Church with you. There is an information display with brochures and flyers about many of our programs and ministries. Please feel free to call me for more info at 404-591-4341, or e-mail at cqualls@spdl.org.

You are our honored guest!

E-mailed or Written Response to Participant Inquiry

Dear _____,

It's good to hear from you. I'm sorry to hear that you are dealing with something so painful in your life, but I am encouraged that you would pick up the phone [or e-mail, or ask a friend] about the Divorce Recovery Program at Second-Ponce de Leon.

Your timing is perfect to ask about the next group.

Our next group is signing up now. You'll want to notice that we start on Wednesday, September 8, at 6:30pm. The link to our web site information is http://www.spdl.org/divorce.html. There, you will find that the sessions will run for eight weeks, meeting each Wednesday night from 6:30 p.m. until 8:00. The cost is $50, which includes your book (we'll provide it on the first night).

Our support group runs twice a year, and participants are often sent to us on referral from their counselors and therapists. Please e-mail me in order to confirm your participation in the group. I would enjoy having you there, and I will stand by in case I can help you with further information. If you have more questions, please feel free to call or e-mail as well.

Welcome to Divorce Recovery at Second-Ponce de Leon Baptist Church!

Here are some tidbits that you might be wondering about:

• Our program begins on Wednesday, February 3, at 6:30 pm and ends by 8:00. We'll be prompt, especially in consideration of our supporting facility personnel. Our meeting place is the Family Life Center in the fireside room. The FLC is the closest building to our parking lot at 2715 Peachtree Road. Please be on time.
• The fee is $50, payable to *Second-Ponce de Leon Baptist Church* (memo line-*Divorce Recovery*). We'll run eight (8) weeks, meeting each Wednesday night. This fee includes your book, *Growing through Divorce*, by Jim Smoke. If you have not had a chance to send your fee ahead of time, please direct it to Charles Qualls, 2715 Peachtree Road, NE, Atlanta, GA 30305. You can also pay as we start.
• Attendance is vital to our experience. You are adults. Attendance cannot be mandated. Part of your journey to recovery is built on your willingness to follow through on commitments you make with others. Your fellow participants will rely on you to be present in order for the group to be all that it can be. Everyone will have something that causes him or her to miss a session. However, please make it a priority to attend as many sessions as possible. Others are counting on you.
• In case of inclement weather, please call our church office. In the event of closure and program cancellation, we will have a special recorded greeting. It will not reference the divorce recovery program specifically, but it will advise you that events are cancelled or altered. Call the number during the afternoon in order to get the most up-to-date information.
• We offer this opportunity for you as a part of your healing. It is available for our church members, but most participants will be from the broader community. As such, we will not push the general program of our church unduly. However, you are welcome at all church activities. We would love to talk further about Second-Ponce de Leon Baptist Church with you. There is an information display with brochures and flyers about many of our programs and ministries.

You are our honored guest!

Divorce Recovery Registration

Winter 2010

Name _____
Address _____
_____
City, State, Zip _____
Daytime Phone ( )_____ Home Phone ( )_____
E-mail _____
Divorce status: (circle one)   Separated   Divorced
How long?_____
Fee paid: Y N

I found the Divorce Recovery Program at Second-Ponce through:
(please check all that apply)

__ banner in front yard of church
__ ad in local publication
__ word-of-mouth (past participants)
__ referral from counselor or therapist
__ church publicity (newsletter, website, announcements etc.)

Endnotes

1. Bill Flanagan, *Developing a Divorce Recovery Ministry: A How-to Manual* (Colorado Springs: NavPress, 1991).

2. Jim Smoke, *Growing through Divorce*, rev. and exp. ed. (Eugene OR: Harvest House, 1995).

3. Harris Law Firm, Denver CO, "U.S. Divorce Statistics (Compiled by the U.S. Census Bureau)" http://www.harrisfamilylaw.com/pdfs/us-divorce-statistics.pdf (accessed 12 June 2011).

4. Diana R. Garland, *Family Ministry: A Comprehensive Guide* (Downers Grove IL: Intervarsity Press, 1999) 543–47.

5. Heidi R. Riggio and Jennifer E. Fite, "Attitudes Toward Divorce: Embeddedness and Outcomes in Personal Relationships," *Journal of Applied Social Psychology* 36 (2006): 2935.

6. Bill Flanagan, Developing a Divorce Recovery Ministry: A How-to Manual (Elgin IL: David C. Cook Publishing, 1994) 14.

7. Miroslav Volf, *Exclusion and Embrace: A Theological Exploration of Identity, Otherness and Reconciliation* (Nashville: Abingdon Press, 1996).

8. Spiritual Capital Initiative at the Yale Center for Faith and Culture, "People: Miroslav Volf," http://spiritualcapital.yale.edu/people-1 (accessed 12 June 2011).

9. Volf, *Exclusion and Embrace*, 92–98.

10. Ibid., 36–37.

11. Ibid.

12. Ibid.

13. Ibid., 140–41.

14. Ibid., 156–66.

15. Miroslav Volf and Tammy Williams, "Narratives of Hope," *Christian Century* 115 (28 January 1998): 86.

16. Jim Smoke, *Growing Through Divorce*, 2d ed. (Eugene OR: Harvest House Publishers, 1995).

17. Bill Flanagan, *Divorce Recovery Workshop: Video Sessions* (Newport Beach CA: St. Andrews Baptist Church, 2000).

18. Harville Hendrix, *Getting the Love You Want: A Guide for Couples* (New York: Henry Holt & Company, 1988) 29–38.

19. Tim VanDuivendyk, *The Unwanted Gift of Grief: A Ministry Approach* (New York: Haworth Pastoral Press, 2006).

20. Elisabeth Kübler-Ross, *On Death and Dying* (New York: Macmillan, 1969).

21. See Henri Nouwen, *The Wounded Healer: Ministry in Contemporary Society* (Garden City NY: Doubleday, 1972).

22. Harville Hendrix, *Getting the Love You Want: A Guide for Couples*, 20th anniversary ed. (New York: H. Holt and Co., 2008).

23. Charles Qualls, "Nurturing the Other Intimacies," Faithworks (March 2003).

24. Warren G. Bennis and Robert Joseph Thomas, Geeks and Geezers (Cambridge: Harvard Business Press, 2002).

SMYTH & HELWYS **HELP!** BOOKS

The Help series is an ongoing collection of guides designed as a resource for ministry leaders and lay people who face challenges within the church. Ranging from tips on preparing a children's sermon to caregiving directions in crisis situations, these books help churches become better equipped for the demands of ministry in today's world.

Crisis Ministry: A Handbook
Daniel G. Bagby

Covering more than 25 crisis pastoral-care situations, this book provides a practical guide for deacons, ministers, and other caregivers.

Drama Ministry: A Guidebook
Nancy Backues, Kerry Beaman, and Wendy Briggs

Drama Ministry: A Guidebook is a one-stop manual for starting, directing, and managing a drama ministry. Lay leaders who have no formal drama training to leaders who are experienced in drama will glean from the authors 25+ years of drama training and experience.

A Christian Educator's Book of Lists
Israel Galindo

This book is a reference manual of basic information that every Christian educator should have on hand. Part basic encyclopedia, part trivia resource, part practical "how to" compilations, part teaching manual, and part general knowledge index, this handbook provides "everything you need to know about Christian education but didn't know where to find."

Divorce Ministry: A Guidebook
Charles Qualls

This book shares with readers the value of establishing a divorce recovery ministry while also offering practical insights on establishing your own unique church-affiliated program. It provides helpful resources to guide you through the emotional and relational issues divorced people often encounter.

SMYTH&HELWYS

SMYTH & HELWYS **HELP!** BOOKS

Help! I'm Leading a Children's Sermon, Vol 1: Advent to Transfiguration Sunday
Marcia Taylor Thompson

This collection of over 70 ready-to-use sermons contains two children's sermons for each Sunday with an emphasis on Scripture, including key verses to be read within the sermon. The sermons invite children to participate in corporate worship in a meaningful, creative way by asking questions and using hands-on activities to explain themes such as hope, forgiveness, repentance, and God's sovereignty.

Help! I Teach Children's Sunday School
B. Max Price

This practical book is a must-read for both first-time and experienced teachers, with information on children from birth through sixth grade. Topics include: A Look at Today's Children, Characteristics of Effective Teachers, Teaching Different Age Groups, Teaching Special Needs Children, What about Discipline?, and much more.

Help! Our Church Is Growing: What to Do When the Old Ways No Longer Work
Mark Phillips

Phillips presents the story of a church in danger of being crushed under the weight of its own growth. This is a survival manual for those whose prayers have been answered.

Help! I'm Leading a Children's Sermon, Vol 2: Lent to Pentecost
Marcia Taylor Thompson

Following the Common Lectionary, there are two sermons for each Sunday with an appendix that contains sermons for Sundays where the Scripture is the same for all three years. The sermons are conversational in nature and focus on Scripture as the source of proclamation.

Help! I Teach Youth Sunday School
Brian Foreman, Bo Prosser, & David Woody

Real-life stories are mingled with information on Youth and their culture, common myths about Sunday School, a new way of preparing the Sunday school lesson, creative teaching ideas, ways to think about growing a class, and how to reach out for new members and reach in to old members.

Marriage Ministry: A Guidebook
Bo Prosser & Charles Qualls

This book is equally helpful for ministers, for nearly/newlywed couples, and for thousands of couples across our land looking for fresh air in their marriages.

Music Ministry: A Guidebook
Donald Clark Measels, ed.

This work is an introduction to church music administration that provides insight into the responsibilities and demands placed on the person who heads the music program of a church.

Visit us online at **www.helwys.com/helpbooks** for helpful topics

www.ingramcontent.com/pod-product-compliance
Lightning Source LLC
Chambersburg PA
CBHW071725090426
42738CB00009B/1882